PRAISE FOR WOMAN'S WAY HOME

Leela is a wayshower for women who are yearning for a more authentic and fulfilling life. Her joy for this work that is her mission jumps out of the pages for the reader and her energy is contagious. As you read this book you'll realize the importance of women truly owning and respecting our bodies in order to fully claim our power and place in this world as leaders.

—Kris Steinnes, Founder of Women of Wisdom Foundation,
and best selling author of Women of Wisdom,
Empowering the Dreams and Spirit of Women.

Leela shows us how to live a sensual, exuberant, embodied life full of satisfaction and delight. She elegantly leads us around pitfalls of body shame, self-hatred and doubt, and shows us how to embrace our shadow and use the power trapped there accessing creative possibilities that we may have never seen before. We see ourselves mirrored in the many stories of those who have taken this journey from confusion, shame and shut down, to a connected and joyful life. She reveals how disconnected we have become from our precious bodies, and shows us how to reconnect to this sacred instrument so we can live a fully embodied life. We come to know we can trust our bodies, our hearts, and our power, and use the wisdom inherent there to guide our lives.

—Joan Heartfield, PhD
Author of *Romancing The Beloved, A Sacred Sexual Journey into Love*

Leela Francis' new, juicy book, Woman's Way Home is inspiring and motivating. There is nothing more important to the planet and people than inspiring and motivating women to fall in love with their power and grace! Bravo.

—Debbie Rosas
Founder and CEO of the Nia Technique, Inc.

Too often, we look to a 'higher power' for guidance and insight. As women, we forget that our true power lies somewhere much lower, in the depths of our wondrous bodies. Leela is a truly natural woman, tuned in deeply to the ancient music of the body. With passion and compassion, she guides her readers into the realms of rooted, sacred embodiment, and into the resting place of our soul's true home.

—Susan Chernak McElroy, author *Heart in the Wild, Animals as Teachers and Healers, Why Buffalo Dance*

Leela Francis has created a clear and concise guidebook for women seeking wholeness and well-being in these turbulent times. Woman's Way Home is a manual for mindfulness and a companion for the journey back to your center.

—Jan Phillips, author of *Divining the Body & The Art of Original Thinking- The Making of a Thought Leader*

Leela Francis' book, Woman's Way Home, is a reflective approach to living an inspired, fulfilling and nourishing life! Her exercises activate a shift in our thinking patterns, raise our behavioral awareness, and help us take action in caring for ourselves as women. She shows us that deep truth is hidden in the layers of our experience and how to turn our struggles into golden nuggets of growth. Her sharing is lively, honest, and full of heart!

—Toni Bergins, Founder & Director of JourneyDance™ International, Transformational Workshops through Dance, Movement, & Theater.

I first met Leela on beautiful Troncones Beach, MX where I was leading an embodiment retreat for "people who love each other". Leela's gentle, loving strength, and her caring ways were a balm to my soul. Hearts open, spirits dance, and souls are embodied when spending time with Leela. Reading her book is worth every minute spent in supporting you and any woman you love along their spiritual path.

—Ellen Watson, Esalen Facilitator & Instructor, Founder of Moving Ventures Non-Profit Educational Institution.

This is an essential guide to your embodied power. Much more than learning to love our bodies, this book shows us the deeper wisdom and power that lies waiting in the cells of our being.

—Christine Stevens, MSW, MT-BC author of
Music Medicine; the Science and Spirit of Healing Yourself with Sound

Woman's Way Home

Navigating Your Path to Embodied Power

LEELA FRANCIS

Balboa Press
A DIVISION OF HAY HOUSE

Copyright © 2013 Leela Francis.
Author Credits: Amazon Best Selling Author, International Speaker

All rights reserved. No part of this book may be used or reproduced by any means, graphic, electronic, or mechanical, including photocopying, recording, taping or by any information storage retrieval system without the written permission of the publisher except in the case of brief quotations embodied in critical articles and reviews.

Balboa Press books may be ordered through booksellers or by contacting:

Balboa Press
A Division of Hay House
1663 Liberty Drive
Bloomington, IN 47403
www.balboapress.com
1-(877) 407-4847

Because of the dynamic nature of the Internet, any web addresses or links contained in this book may have changed since publication and may no longer be valid. The views expressed in this work are solely those of the author and do not necessarily reflect the views of the publisher, and the publisher hereby disclaims any responsibility for them.

The author of this book does not dispense medical advice or prescribe the use of any technique as a form of treatment for physical, emotional, or medical problems without the advice of a physician, either directly or indirectly. The intent of the author is only to offer information of a general nature to help you in your quest for emotional and spiritual well-being. In the event you use any of the information in this book for yourself, which is your constitutional right, the author and the publisher assume no responsibility for your actions.

Any people depicted in stock imagery provided by Thinkstock are models, and such images are being used for illustrative purposes only.
Certain stock imagery © Thinkstock.

ISBN: 978-1-4525-7404-2 (sc)
ISBN: 978-1-4525-7406-6 (hc)
ISBN: 978-1-4525-7405-9 (e)

Library of Congress Control Number: 2013908231

Printed in the United States of America.

Balboa Press rev. date: 10/3/2013

TABLE OF CONTENTS

PREFACE xi

FOREWORD xv

ACKNOWLEDGEMENTS xvii

INTRODUCTION xix

HOW TO USE THIS BOOK xxv

1. Centers, Textures, and Lenses
The Dimensions of Living Vividly 1

POWER CENTERS
The Wisdom that Lives in Your Body

2. Sensual Power
Remembering your Body as a Temple 19

3. Emotional Power
Mastering the Rich World of Your Emotions 49

4. Intuitive Power
Dancing Your Higher-Self 68

TEXTURES
Mature Energy Management

5. Sense
Awareness is the Foundation of Your Journey 91

6. Ground
Cultivate Presence and Your Earth Body 110

7. Mobilize
Meaning that Motivates and Ignites Your Life 128

8. Harness
Sustain Expansion: Make More Out of Less 144

9. Express
Celebrate Truth and the Key to Intimacy 166

LENSES
Portals to Wisdom

10. Lenses
How We Look Determines What We See 187

11. Somatic Lens
Resource Your Body's Truth 191

12. Creative Lens
Discover the Gift 199

13. Spiritual Lens
Awaken Transpersonal Power 205

14. Dancing the Solar System
Explore with Your Body 210

CONCLUSION 225

ABOUT THE AUTHOR 227

THE VIVIDLY WOMAN EXPERIENCE................................229

SUGGESTED READING 233

SUPPORT RESOURCES 237

INDEX..241

PREFACE

Sacred Homecoming

Welcome, Sister. You've found your way to the first pages of a book called *Woman's Way Home*. I have to assume this means home is something that's been evading you, that you're aware enough to know that a sense of home within yourself is sorely lacking, and that you crave a safe and secure route back there. Most likely, you're longing to know where home is and how to find it again if you lose your way in the future.

I wouldn't doubt that you're feeling alone, and lost, and awfully homesick for your true soul—essence. That you've arrived at the conclusion that if you're ever going to find home—the truth of who you really are—you have to be willing to set out on the journey to get there. I am devoted to you and your journey. I've seen that while we must each navigate our own inner terrain to find our way home and get comfortable being there, sisterhood along the way is very helpful.

This book is an invitation to get you home. It promises to aid you in releasing the chains of self-judgment, fear, and self-hate, to help you midwife your own rebirth, to assist you to be in authentic dialogue with your body, to discover the light and the shadow of your inner being, and to make love to your life on a daily basis. But first, you have to be willing to acknowledge your pain, the feelings of being lost, and the value in having support and guidance. Congratulations, by finding this book you've made it over that first big hurdle and from here on in you can expect to discover the tools that will help make your way more accessible, intriguing, and fruitful.

I first heard the expression *divine homesickness* many years ago from my therapist and teacher, Mary Pinnager. Mary and I worked together on and off over a period of about sixteen years. It was with her that I discovered what it meant to attend to my soul's longing to be truly cared for and to value the journey home to my soul-essence. It was only in vividly tasting a homesickness of my soul that I could honor that there was a road I would need to tread in order to truly come home.

During those years of abundant psycho-spiritual anguish, interspersed with scant periods of relief from the suffering, accompanied by spurts of awakening and expansion, I received much of the personal training and soul awakening that has come to be the accumulated wisdom found in the Vividly Woman body of work that is the Embodied Leader Training. There were other teachers and trainings along the way, but it was mainly with the help of my teacher, therapist, and friend (for Mary and her longtime partner at the time were also dear friends) that I had the blessing to devote myself to my own healing, with Mary serving as a constant and a rudder to my chaotic flailing and colorful, dramatic dance of life.

At the time, I had no idea what all those years might one day amount to. When in the midst of personal struggle, it's hard to imagine there will actually be a light at the end of the tunnel. I thrashed about, trying desperately to get my footing in a life that seemed to serve me up a relentless helping of challenges and *dark nights*, especially around my primary relationships, infertility, a failed adoption, and career hurdles. When I look back, I can see that while I was learning important self-awareness tools to guide others and myself home, I was also learning how to reverently acknowledge my own inner turmoil. It was her quality of empathy that Mary modeled for me that I have been most grateful to be the recipient of. Mary affirmed for me that my suffering was not wrong or bad or indulgent. She helped me take my first steps as a woman who was honoring her way home and would one day be able to midwife many others on that path.

Were it not for Mary's loving and sacred container those sixteen years, I would likely have believed that my challenges were unusual and unique. I would have suffered in silence and been armored against the pain. I would have hidden further and further away from the truth of my soul and I would have built more and more of a façade to hide the shame of my inner struggles. Mary's wisdom and devoted heart helped me to witness all of the above tendencies in myself but not be consumed by them.

Today, I'm blessed to carry the sensitivity, insight, and awareness that allows me to sense other women who are aching in similar ways, and to help them along their path home. I'm keenly attuned to that shrinking back into oneself, of the fear of being seen in one's pain, at being judged for weakness and the shame of inner emotional insanity. I see it in the eyes, the belly, the shoulders, and the knees; I hear it in their words and silence. I have gathered in enough sacred safe circles to know that no one's story is unique and no one's suffering is wrong, and yet women are still prisoners of the belief that they are all alone and no one will understand and accept them if they know the truth.

My heart aches for the lengths to which we've strived not to be found out. The fear of not being loved has pushed us so far away from our authentic truth that there is little left of the true self in our relationships anyway! "Who do I need to be so that x will love me?" This question has become the background music to our lives so that we barely hear it at all anymore.

On my way to a Vividly Woman training a while back I had the good fortune of bumping into Mary in the supermarket. It had been several years since we had last met. It was an auspicious and meaningful time to see her. It was hard to reconcile the reality that so many years of inner struggle could now have me running my own training program for women's emotional healing and spiritual growth. At our chance meeting in the fresh produce section, I felt a profoundly sentimental appreciation for who Mary had been on my path and I told her so. After we spent a few moments catching up we were each on our way. Later in the day, still deeply touched by this encounter, I recalled that many of those sixteen years, and still today, I judged myself for how "fucked up" my life used to be and wondered what the hell she must have thought of me. Then I got it; she was your therapist, Leela, of course she was intimately privy to the tossing and turning of your life just as I am now to those I work with. And do I think them fucked up? No, I just hold the space for whatever presents itself, trusting the perfection of the dance that each of us choreographs for ourselves so we can heal, learn, expand and then eventually serve as a *way—shower* for others on their glorious and meaningful woman's way home.

FOREWORD

All women of the world – survivors of violence in destitute slums, victims of genocide in the desolate displacement camps, suburban moms, every woman stranded in poverty, the women-in-training at high schools and colleges and those privileged with a life of luxuries – all of us face the same life-defining questions:

How do we think about the life we have been given, a life blessed or cursed by timing, place and family, none of which we chose?

What is the purpose of our presence here and now?

How do we embrace and manifest our unique gifts?

Where do we turn for the "hand up" that enables our shift from confusion and despair to devotion and hope?

What is our contribution to the upwelling sisterhood of women?

For each of us, the answers arrive at different times, sometimes after pain and sorrow, hopefully accompanied by relief and a sense of greater freedom. For our life to have meaning and direction, the questions – and the answers – form the essence of our link with the rest of humanity.

Our lives are shorter, of more urgent mandate, than we usually care to admit. It is never too late to begin, or deepen, an honest investigation of the big questions – especially when important opportunities present themselves.

This book is one such opportunity. I recommend you immerse yourself in the wisdom offered here and allow it to open your mind, heart and soul. Leela Francis models a devotion and service to women that in and of itself inspires us to wake up to our inherent wisdom and the gifts of our life journey so that we can be a light for each other.

The power of a woman fully, vibrantly on her path, imbued with richness, is the power needed to transform the world, day by day, into the nurturing habitat we want it to be.

I wish you joyful success on your journey.

Susan Burgess-Lent

Author, Journalist, Speaker,
Warrior for Women's Rights
Executive Director, Women's Centers International.

ACKNOWLEDGEMENTS

I have all my teachers to thank for helping me compile the wisdom I offer in this book. For the courage to share my stories and find the right words and organization of those I feel great gratitude for my editor, Lynne Blackman.

Amongst the memorable and life influencing teachers I've been blessed to know and study with are Debbie Rosas, Zeta Gaudet, Mary Pinnager, Carol Brophie, Judith and Jerry Fewster, Liz Faller, Jaime Ewen, Sandra Samartino, Ann Mortiphee, Richard and Donna Dryer, Emilie Conrad, Susan Harper, Marion Rosen, Toni Bergins, Wilbert Alix, Andrea Juhan, Banafshe Sayad, Belisa Amaro, Regine, Shakti Mai, Jean Bolen, Yuki Rioux, Mrs. Paul, Mary Beetles, Hadia, and Mrs. Shapiro, my nursery school teacher who wore white patent leather go-go boots

There are many whose lives have impacted the meaning and depth of my own. Besides the formal teachers that I listed above, these women effortlessly shared their life wisdom and introduced me to many important places in myself, without which this book would never have been written.

Judith, thank you for your years of devotion to your own healing and sanity and the risks you took to empower yourself. Pammy, thank you for opening my eyes to a depth of human honesty that helped carve my evolution. Betty, you introduced me to sacred space and constantly provided it for me when I most needed a soft place to land. Dhyana, your life dance and autonomy gave me a role model of what a woman can be and still have a profoundly deep heart. Joyce and Judy, the reality of life and relationships was birthed for me through you. Kara and Randi, your sisterhood and devotion to the path of Vividly Woman have buoyed me immeasurably, thank you for answering my call. Diana, thank you for standing by my side behind the scenes and working your butt off to make it all look just right, and Greg, thank you for showing me another way, for loving me, and always encouraging me to follow my true heart. Nancy, thank you for modeling and nourishing me with love and affection. Alan, thank you for being an amazing big brother, for literally saving my life, and for always being there for me when I need you. Mum, for loving me from the womb and being a mother I ached to make proud.

Thank you to the soul and essence of Lallashwari, whose naked dance has been with me in every circle, whose passionate longing for truth is in the heart of every woman I meet, and whose reverent light shines on all of my days.

INTRODUCTION

Embodiment is something I started out facilitating before I knew myself what it truly was. While I knew what it felt and looked like to be embodied (truly inhabiting my body instead of just dragging it around with me by default) and what it felt and looked like to not be embodied, I really didn't have the understanding to be able to speak about it or tell anyone how they could be more embodied themselves.

I was however bestowed with a natural ability to inspire embodied presence, through the way that I naturally lived in my own body. My love and passion and indulgence in dance and movement, and even the way I carried myself in my everyday life, attracted to me individuals who wanted what I seemed to have. I in turn was inspired to help them find it in themselves.

What a gift! All I had to do was show up and dance, and I would be serving others. How sweet is that?

That did seem like a fortunate set of circumstances, since I loved to dance, and practically lived for it. Unfortunately it didn't turn out to be enough for the inquiring minded, embodied soul that I am. I yearned to understand, with my mind, what it is that constitutes embodied living, how I could improve my transmission of that gift and wisdom to be of even greater service, and why it was even important? Put simply, I wanted to become conscious. Along with raising my own consciousness, I longed to support others on that road as well. My challenge became to substantiate and justify the healing work of dance, movement, and embodied psycho-spirituality so that doubting minds would feel inclined to take part, to drink the Kool-Aid so to speak, that was bringing so much deliciousness to my own existence.

Serving women to awaken them to the power and pleasure of their sensual bodies through dance, nature and ritual was a passion that seemed unquenchable for me. Spurred by firsthand physical abuse I'd experienced by my own partner, I trained and worked as a volunteer rape-line crisis worker, and then as a counselor for battered and abused women and children in a women's shelter. I'd touched these issues in my own life and held space for others to heal in theirs. I didn't think I could become even more smitten with promoting women's embodied power until an issue of global importance grabbed my attention. The issue that I speak of is women, our sisters, who are victims of horrific sexual violence as a consequence of war. I began to learn about places like Rwanda and Bosnia and where it's still happening today, women's bodies and souls being attacked, raped, and tortured in places like Darfur and the Congo.

Along with my tremendous grief, I felt great confusion because while these women, who have little means, education, and opportunity are brutally victimized, and tortured, the sacredness of their sensuality violated, we women of the developed world, living in our privileged wealthy culture, commit a similarly debilitating violence and betrayal against ourselves by ignoring and dishonoring our own sacred sensuality, day after day, in how we organize and design our lives and priorities.

My compulsion to guide and inspire my sisters locally largely grew out of the pain I felt for my less advantaged sisters who were suffering globally. I knew in my own heart and soul that the greatest difference we can make on this planet is to come home to the blessing and the wisdom of our own bodies. Then came the need to carve out the path to get there and make it conceptual enough so that I could convey it to elicit curiosity and credibility. That is when my passion and service became activism, and I claimed my power to effect change.

In my quest to support women, I trusted that the theoretical wisdom would come in time. There were many seasons of doubt along the way, but fortunately I gradually became more and more clear. After years of dedication to this field of study and my own personal expansion and conscious embodiment the moving parts clicked into place, opening the space for more aha moments that allow for ever greater insights and understandings.

The beauty of the Vividly Woman System laid out, discussed, and explored in these pages, is that long after you have attended a Vividly Woman Training, or even if you never attend, or hope to one day, you will have the seeds of what it takes to begin living more intimately in your own skin, and become the midwife of your own soul-body, which is ultimately my greatest wish for each and every woman on this planet.

We have spent so much time living up to other people's and society's standards that we've almost completely disconnected from our own deepest and authentic truth. If there is anything that is at the root of the rampant depression, poor health, and lack of fulfillment experienced by so many women, it is this one startling and unfortunate reality: We chronically dishonor our truth and ourselves. Even though we're constantly acquiescing to the needs and expectations of others in order to win love and approval, the actual end result does not enhance our well-being. This constant betrayal of our selves to fit in, get along with others, and be accepted, is causing profound anguish, depression, anxiety, and disenchantment among women. With all the wealth and blessings that we have to boast, we are still walking around feeling like something important is missing. This sense of loss is the privileged woman's version of suffering. Vividly Woman education, community and training are devoted to us suffering less and living our lives as a celebration more.

The missing something is the experience of inhabiting our bodies—living congruently between our hearts, minds, and bodies. If self-betrayal is my habitual way of being, it will show up in any one of the above areas, and will always reveal itself in how I feel in my body, which gets translated in everything I do, say, and attempt to achieve.

I believe that the paradigm shift of women coming home to our greatest power cannot take place without an embodied wisdom that radiates from within. Without it we continue to perpetuate the old values and paradigm that has women acting like men. Men are certainly beautiful. But let's leave being a man to the men, and let's be women, body, self, and soul! The Dalai Lama tells us "our planet will be saved by the western woman." This is a wise and powerful statement. But as far as I'm concerned, if this planet is going to be saved by western women pretending to men, I'm headed to another planet!

This book is for women hungering to live in synch with their truth and offers a theoretical companion to support the experiential journey they must each make in order to birth themselves as embodied leaders. While I believe that experiential learning is necessary for sustained personal/spiritual growth and energetic expansion, I see the value of engaging our minds in service of our bodies. The Vividly Woman System and its components outlined in this book are happily available as tools to deepen every woman's intimacy with herself and to help her dance into an embodied version of power that can be a path for healthier, more successful, and genuinely fulfilling living.

I've spent years of devoted study in the field of embodiment and holding space for thousands of people to wake up to their inner aliveness, aching to be ignited. I've seen that embodiment is accessible to every one of us if we feel that it's safe to live in our body. Getting to that safe place and learning how to spend more time there is what I invite you to discover in this book and then to live that as a radiant expression of embodied leadership.

I am deeply grateful to the many women who have taken part in the Vividly Woman Embodied Leader and Vividly Woman Embodiment Coach Trainings especially those who generously shared their own stories to help put the information here in context, making it easier to understand and apply in one's own life. I have been blessed to know you all as my teachers, my sisters, and my cherished friends in this great and sacred circle of life that we are all dancing together.

The ideas and insights I've set out here for you to chew on are not the beginning or end of this embodiment story. Your own unique experiences and insights are a wonderful contribution to the ever-expanding body of knowledge on the topic of embodiment. Together as women we are growing this collective feminine awakening, one beautiful, sacred body at a time!

HOW TO USE THIS BOOK

If you're new to the world of Vividly Woman you may find the terms and concepts presented here different or unfamiliar. The greatest value you can harvest from these pages will be learning to identify where these terms and concepts show up in your life so that you can move them from the conceptual to the experienced; that's what embodiment is.

I suggest that after Chapter 1, you read each of the following chapters on its own. Once you've completed a chapter, visit the *"Stimulator"* link provided at the end of that chapter where you'll be invited to download an audio, video or written workbook excerpt that will help you to further deepen your embodiment of that chapter's content. You can also refer to chapter 14 where you'll find a movement practice and music ideas for chapters 2 through 13.

Please take time to give the information in the chapter you've just read time to simmer and sink in. Let the ideas, stories, and information find their interface with you and your life. This is how you'll have an intimate and rich experience of the system that Vividly Woman offers, an abundance of precious wisdom that is the accumulation of many schools of thought, trainings, and teachers that I've had the blessing to study and circle with.

Start to notice how each of the centers, textures, and lenses is showing up in your life, past and present, and how you might weave them into your future. Let these insights arise naturally in the course of your daily life. Spend some time journaling your reflections to further bring conscious awareness to your journey with this work.

If you find you'd like to explore the ideas in more depth with the assistance of a Vividly Woman Embodiment Coach please reach out to us at http://vividlywoman.com/certified-coaches

Dance, Lalla, with nothing on
but air: Sing, Lalla,
wearing the sky.
Look at this glowing day!
What clothes
could be so beautiful, or
more sacred?

~Lalla

> "…women gathering together in groups and telling the truth of their lives can actually change the world."
> ~ Jean Bolen

CHAPTER 1

Centers, Textures, and Lenses

The Dimensions of Living Vividly

We are a small group of women sitting together in a sacred circle. We've gathered items that represent the four elements: earth, water, air, and fire, for a central altar that holds the space of the sacred center of our circle, the place where all our respective stories become one. We've joined together for the weekend, to share and explore our soulful, woman-ful connection to life and deepen the meaning of our existence.

Many of the women who sit in this circle, are here for the very first time. They feel nervous, hesitant; some even feel scared or terrified. "Why did I come here" you can almost hear their thoughts in the silence. "There are so many other things I could be doing this weekend. What's the point of a woman's circle anyway?"

Their nervousness is practically palpable. Many of these women have done lots of risky things in their life. They've traveled, raised families, held powerful positions in business and policy making organizations, and sought ways to grow and expand, so it's not as if they're strangers to living outside the box. But sitting in a sacred circle with a bunch of women, most of them strangers, is still foreign and threatening. Maybe it's because of the many years we've mistrusted other women, maybe it's because intimacy and vulnerability are scary, maybe it's because they can sense something big is about to shift in them. Whatever the reasons for their fears and concerns, they are clearly ready to move beyond them, because they are here.

Firsthand experience is the best way to learn. It gets woven into your cellular being and takes you through the resistance and fabricated excuses of the mind. Weekends like these are designed primarily to get beneath the rational mind's understanding into the depth and mystery that lies behind and beyond the stories we weave as interpretations.

In order to make sense of the why and place the wisdom and insights in context so that they can be more effectively applied to your life, a methodology works wonders. For a group who are landing in strange territory like a sacred woman's circle for the first time, a travel guide that describes and charts out the journey can be invaluable in helping us to navigate the process that lies ahead.

The Vividly Woman System of Somatic Awakening, the nuts and bolts of the Vividly Woman Embodied Leader Training, has three main dimensions. These three dimensions: centers, textures, and lenses, are the tools that we use to orient ourselves, to resource our own deeper wisdom, and to organize our inquiries and investment of life energy. Each of these dimensions stands on its own and simultaneously interweaves with the others creating what we call on a schematic level, the Vividly Woman Solar System (VWSS). The diagram on the next page maps it out visually for you.

The Vividly Woman Solar System

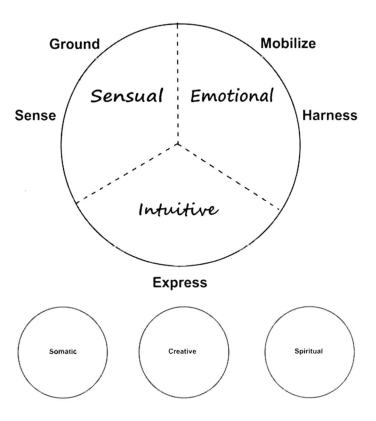

This system is a way of making it easier for you to explore the wilderness of your soul-body, so that you can learn from its wild mysteries. The VWSS supports you to embrace your body as a canvas for creative change, so that how you are in your body can help you grow and change in ways that will bring you greater peace and fulfillment in all aspects of your life.

Power Centers

At the heart of the Vividly Woman Solar System are the three feminine power centers. They sit at the center of the system, like the sun sits at the center of our earth's solar system, a fiery hot globe around which the planets (Vividly Woman textures) constellate.

We sometimes refer to the three feminine power centers as the three inner fountains of feminine wisdom. This alternative name is less static and captures the sensual abundance that's an important aspect of them. The centers or fountains are the Sensual, Emotional, and Intuitive. They correspond to the pelvis, the chest, and head respectively. This means that each center's wisdom is primarily embodied in that area of the body, but is not limited to just that area. That's why the lines between the respective centers in the diagram of the Vividly Woman Solar System are broken instead of solid, so that the wisdom and energy can flow between them.

Our body is an interactive, integrated whole made up of many parts and systems that function because of their interrelatedness. It's important to remember that each center's wisdom is primarily embodied in that area of the body, but not exclusively. For instance, Emotional Power is mainly accessed and stored in the area of the heart which sits in the chest, however, emotional energy certainly also resides at the level of the throat, where expression is resourced, or can be profoundly connected to our sexuality, at the level of the pelvis, where Sensual Power and wisdom are prominent. While it can be helpful to know where in your body you can directly access your Emotional Power, it's equally as important to know that emotions surf through your tissues and can and do affect your entire body. Sensual aliveness and intuitive knowing work the very same way, especially for women, whose bodies are a universe of erogenous potential.

WOMEN'S EROGENOUS ZONES

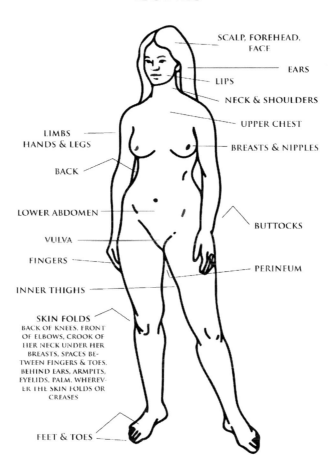

For the sake of learning we focus at first on how, for instance, Sensual Power lives in and is resourced in the pelvic area, but once we're familiar with the sensations and textures of Sensual Power within us, we can begin to appreciate and enjoy how Sensual Power dances in every cell and fiber in our beautiful body and will move and change from day to day, from moment to moment, dependent on many other factors including emotion, environment, and interpersonal dynamics—not to mention physiology.

Power

 It's not that we don't have enough power, it's that we aren't at home with what we do have.

Let's explore the concept of power for a moment. What is power? Is it possible that some people have more power than others do? I've often heard someone say "So and so is a very powerful woman or man." I personally don't believe that anyone has any more power than anyone else. I believe that we all have the same access to power. It's what we prioritize as power and how we harness power that makes the difference. In addition, each of us is more or less comfortable with our own power. Being in our power may be a threat to the life we've created, the relationships we've committed to and built our lives around, personally and professionally.

When you feel like you don't have the power that you think you need, it may just be that you're not at home with your power, and that you don't know where to resource it from within yourself. "I know I'm powerful, but I'm afraid to access my own power," Carla, one of the Sisters in the VW community, wrote to me a few months before attending the week-long Vividly Woman Mexico retreat called Sacred Sensual Splendor.

I think hers is a sentiment that many women feel, but often aren't conscious of. Instead, we think we lack power and the right to it. The importance of the distinction between not having power, and just not being comfortable with it, is that we discover that the judgments and beliefs of not being enough, that so many women carry, are debunked and laid to rest. It's not that we don't have enough power, it's that we aren't at home with what we do have. As far as I'm concerned it's a far less daunting, and a far more feminine task to acquire the comfort than it is to believe that we need to amp up the voltage!

"This last two and a half months [since attending Dance Your Power] have been incredible, as I have certainly been walking in a different kind of power. One that, once given permission came so naturally to me," another VW Sister, Saria, shared.

Getting well acquainted with the feminine centers of power within you, claiming their own unique expression through your body and your life, will give you authentic access to your own inner power living right inside of you. You'll discover that looking within yourself for wisdom, instead of outside of you, is the quickest and most effective path to power.

Unfortunately, most of us have grown up believing that the power centers presented here are actually our weaknesses instead of our strengths. "Don't be too sexual, don't be so emotional, don't say what you really think, and always look for proof outside instead of from inside yourself." These are the kinds of things that have become so ingrained in us that we hardly notice them anymore. We operate at the mercy of these often-covert beliefs and values, and they unconsciously run our lives, depriving us of our well-being and ultimately of our inherent aliveness and potential.

The centers are places of energy abundance in the body that also correspond to the three feminine chakras (yogic energy centers). The organs that live in each area correspond to the characteristics of that center and clearly contribute to the energetic there. E.g. the ovaries and genitals live in the area where our Sensual Power resides, the second chakra. These organs play a starring role in our potential for sexual and sensual pleasure, which is one component of our sensual life expression, our Sensual Power.

For the purposes of embodiment, we access personal information through felt Sense awareness in each of these centers. An example of this is listening inwardly for sensations in the heart area to learn how we authentically feel about something. We also effect change in our life pertaining to each of these issues, sensual, emotional, and intuitive, by mobilizing and exploring with each of these body areas. E.g. moving our head and neck to unlock Intuitive Power.

Over the next three chapters we'll explore each of the centers closely, one per chapter. You'll come to intimately know the hows and whys of your Sensual Power, your Emotional Power, and your Intuitive Power, which will inspire further personal inquiry, which is the highest ideal of this book. As I mentioned in the introduction, the ideas and insights I've set out here for you to explore are not the final word on the topic of embodiment, more accurately, this is a place to inspire greater thirst for self-inquiry.

Textures

The textures are landmarks in the Vividly Woman System of Embodiment, planets that constellate around or relate to the power centers. They guide us to understand and embody the dance of energy in our life. This energetic pattern is always at play, though most often unconsciously. Becoming aware of how the textures play out in your life will give you mastery over them so that you begin to recognize your habits and can then make conscious choices in your own best interest. The textures are: Sense, Ground, Mobilize, Harness, and Express. And while I list them here in a linear way, they actually exist in a circular continuum that is always renewing itself.

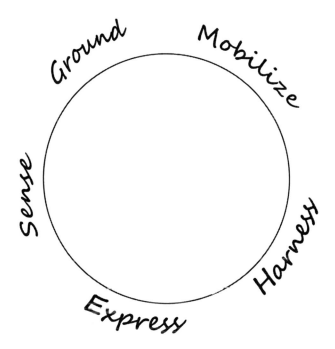

They're called textures because they each have a characteristic felt Sense quality within us, which is unique. Your felt Sense quality of Ground will be different than mine and what is essential is that you become acquainted with it in your own body. One of the Vividly Woman trainings, Embody Self Love Intensive, gives you a profound experience of this. Through psycho-spiritual practices such as dyads, trance dance, and eco-therapy, we excavate our long-buried respective truths, pertaining to each of the textures, thereby reclaiming their authentic essence in our lives.

When you read the chapters on each of the textures you'll likely see some of yourself in each of them, however you'll most likely see yourself more in one at a certain time in your life. This is very handy information. It will help you to look at the patterns and habits in your life and understand more of what makes you tick and why your life is the way it is. If you want to see your life change, just look at the textures to see where you need to go next in order to graduate forward in the continuum.

For instance, about two years ago I identified myself as a Mobilize kind of person. I would have many balls in the air at once, busy with making lots of projects happen and always taking on new ones without thinking things through before I started or committed myself. It was exciting and creative and kept me engaged. Eventually, I started to feel overwhelmed, and began resenting how much of my time was being consumed, and how the results of my efforts weren't meeting my expectations. With this awareness, I understood that Mobilize energy is great to have, but unless I also engage the energy of Ground, I would keep spinning my wheels and never achieve the blessings of self-replenishing energy that is the essence of Harness, the next texture after Mobilize. Now, two years later, I'm much more picky about how I devote my time. I say no a lot more and my actions are self-sustaining instead of exhausting. I've graduated from Mobilize to Harness, but both textures, like all five, are important and of great value in our lives.

In Chapters 5-9 you'll taste each of the textures one by one to get a delicious awareness of each of their gifts, wisdom, and life giving inspiration.

Lenses

The lenses that we use in the Vividly Woman Solar System are the Somatic, Spiritual, and Creative. A lens, as you know, is a device that we look through in order to see more accurately. The quality and type of lens we use will, of course, affect how and what we see, giving access to perspectives and nuances specific to the quality of that lens.

 Try a new twist on an old issue to open doors and aid the evolution of your consciousness.

We use each of the three lenses mentioned above to shift our perspective in order to see differently so that we can gain awareness and insight previously unavailable to us. Instead of continuing to look at things the way we always have, we gain a new twist on an old issue, which opens doors and aids evolution of consciousness.

Here's an example: Terry was feeling stuck with regard to her new company. Just having launched a business in health care, she was hesitant to make the cold calls she knew were necessary to kick start the business. Using the Somatic Lens, we asked her body what it had to say about this fear and hesitation. When she went inside to get the answer, she sensed a quivering in her belly, a little girl part of her that experienced terror and dread. "I thought I had healed this wounded little girl!" she lamented. "After years of time and money, I thought I'd peeled all the layers away around the abuses in my childhood." The Somatic Lens helped us identify the part of her that was holding her back, and also the judgment, resentment, and rejection she was inflicting on this innocent, fragile part of her. As she reclaimed and embraced this little girl, she became aware that it is precisely this part of her that can help her make authentic, genuine, trusting connections with potential clients in her health care business.

In Chapters 11, 12, and 13, you'll read about how each of the lenses offers a unique portal into any issue about which you might have lost hope after weeks, months, or years of banging your head against a wall. Not only did your spirit (and your head) feel worn and withered, but the issue did not get resolved. You just continued the inner struggle. The lenses are a blessing that can support you to expand possibility, deepen wisdom, and, most of all, relieve suffering. Who doesn't want more of that?

Using three simple questions, a whole world will open itself to you and instead of frustration you'll be feeling empowered and renewed:

Somatic Lens—What does my body have to say about this?

Creative Lens—What is the creative opportunity for me here?

Spiritual Lens—How am I being used by spirit?

In the lens chapters we'll explore the value of each of these lenses and how the lens questions can be a portal on the road from victimhood to embodied power.

Embodiment vs. Understanding

Embodiment means the ability to resource your body's wisdom for truth. While your head is capable of great interpretive skills and story weaving commentary, your body is only able to deliver truthful information about what's happening now.

Looking to the body for its wisdom on whatever is going on will always give you pure, accurate, and uncluttered truth. Where embodiment relies on integration and assimilation, understanding remains purely conceptual or theoretical.

Out of habit, avoidance, and shame, we are masters at leaving our body. Our minds split off and become fragmented from our bodies, resulting in a chronically disembodied state of being. "The theft of the body" is a term I heard author Clarissa Pinkola Estes use in her audio book, *The Joyous Body,* and I think it well describes an epidemic among women especially. It's common for a woman to only pay attention to her body when in pain or when she finds some fault with it. Embodiment can teach you how to get back home into your body, to notice when you're not home (when we've abandoned ship so to speak), how to get back on board, over and over again, until eventually we discover it's actually safe to stay here.

Live events are a great vehicle for learning through your body. Workbooks can be effective as well. In this book I'll offer you many concepts and at least one experiential exercise per chapter as an opportunity to take those concepts into action in your body so that they become felt Sense experiences. You'll have your own insights and aha's through these practices that will expand your body of truth about embodiment. Please feel very welcome to share those with me as I continue to compile personal experiences and anecdotes that will help make this information more accessible for students and readers.

Embodiment is a way of having a felt Sense experience in your body first, in order to manifest that quality in your life. I often say, "The body is a wilderness of self-discovery and a canvas for creative change." Owning and living in your body for its tremendous wisdom helps you graduate from using your body like a machine to inhabiting it as a temple. Compare the wheels and cogs of a machine to the exotic sculptural beauty of a temple, and you can easily imagine the difference. What do you want to be living? For a woman, the temple version of living is a big step forward into living a richer every day existence. I know firsthand that this will give you ample cause for celebration both personally and professionally.

But I've also lived at the opposite extreme.

There was a time in my own life when, as the stepmom of three teenage boys, I felt helplessly surrounded by testosterone and unable to maintain the essence of the feminine in my life. The machine version of life was all around me. Nowhere, could I find the longed-for inspiration for honoring of the body as a temple that I instinctively knew was more resonant and nourishing for me. I sunk into a state of emotional and psychological depression during that time and despite the outward appearance of a fulfilling life, I was in fact suffering in a deep and dark despair. I wasn't able to make sense of why I was so sullen at the time, I just knew something was very wrong with the way I was feeling and wanted desperately to shift it.

Looking back, I know that experience was a gift that drove me to seek out a more embodied existence closer to nature. It was the catalyst that inspired me to create my home on a tropical beach in Mexico where I would come to do so much of the deep personal work that was my birthing of the Vividly Woman Embodied Leader Training.

It was here, on the wild and thundering shores of a remote Mexican village that I discovered what the true meaning of feminine power and embodied leadership is: being a leader because of your relationship with your body instead of in spite of or at the expense of it.

There are several important reasons why this is so important:

1. Our physical health is ultimately the determining factor in the quality of our life.
2. Our comfort and ease with our body is a radiant expression of our relationship with our self. It speaks volumes to our audience, customers, and clients.
3. Our relationships are the first to be influenced by our integrity or lack of it. Our integrity in our relationship with our body inspires integrity in all our relationships.
4. Our body is a consistent source of truth vs. ego. Truth is a clear and profound pathway to happiness and peace, while lack of truth perpetuates suffering.

The Vividly Woman Solar System mapped out in the pages that follow are a guide to support you on your way to acknowledging yourself as an embodied leader and celebrating the passion for aliveness that's aching to be danced in every cell of your being.

Chapter 1 Summary: Centers, Textures, and Lenses

~ The Vividly Woman Solar System conceptually maps out the Vividly Woman methodology and has three dimensions: the power centers, the textures and the lenses.

~ The three power centers are Sensual, Emotional, and Intuitive.

~ We all have the same access to power. It's what we prioritize, how we harness and how comfortable we are with our own power that makes the difference.

~ The textures are Sense, Ground, Mobilize, Harness, and Express.

~ Textures are landmarks in the Vividly Woman system of embodiment; planets that constellate around or relate to the power centers. They guide us to understand and embody the dance of energy in our life.

~ The three lenses are Somatic, Creative, and Spiritual.

~ We use each of the three lenses to shift our perspective in order to see differently so that we can gain awareness and insight previously unavailable to us.

~ Embodiment relies on integration and assimilation, while understanding remains purely conceptual or theoretical.

~ Embodied leadership means that you are a leader because of your relationship with your body instead of in spite of or at the expense of it.

POWER CENTERS

The Wisdom that Lives in Your Body

The Vividly Woman Solar System

"My body is burning with the fire of love. It seems that all the sins and sorrows and cravings of my life have been used as fuel for the fire of this love."
~ Mirabai

CHAPTER 2

Sensual Power

Remembering your Body as a Temple

Sensual: Pertaining to the senses of the physical body and its relationship to all the other realms

Sensual Power: Honoring the felt Sense experience of the physical body

Claiming and living our Sensual Power empowers us to have good health, healthy sexuality, and sensual pleasure in everyday experiences.

It would be difficult to have all of the above and be completely disconnected from your body. You might work out three times a week and have a beautiful body by the media's standards, but that doesn't guarantee that you're actually fully enjoying your body on a sensual level. In fact, most people who are doing the typical gym workout are treating their body like a mechanical instrument, instead of as a precious exotic temple that houses their divinity. Give some thought for a moment to what and how it is you want to be living: mechanically or exotically?

Sensual Power is the gift of savoring your connection to the richness of life, pleasure, and the joy of living in a body. Being embodied means truly living in your body by virtue of that intimate connection.

Living in your body, consciously inhabiting your body temple is necessary if you want to hear its truth, deeply and vividly connect with the sensual world of nature, and savor the deliciousness of each and every precious moment.

The Sensual Body

The word sensual is, as it implies, of the senses. Our senses are a faculty of our physical body in relationship to the world around us and inside of us. The way we use sensual body in the world of Vividly Woman is as a combination of the physical and the spiritual. When I refer to my physical body, I'm referring to my anatomical structure and all the parts contained therein. This is my body as a machine. When I refer to my sensual body, I'm referring to my physical body as a vessel for my spiritual body, a temple that houses the divine within me.

When I speak about my own fitness, I prefer to use the term sensual fitness instead of physical fitness. Sensual fitness is where I not only strengthen my physical body, but it's also where I strengthen my practice of listening respectfully to the truth of what my whole self needs instead of overriding it with what I want it to need. I've hurt myself doing that in the past. The more I practice listening, the more easily I hear what my body wants me to know about how to keep her healthy, strong, and nourished. Thinking that I could hear my body without taking the time to really listen is kind of absurd and yet it seems that's what a lot of us do much of the time. In Chapter 11 Somatic Lens, we'll look at the Vividly Woman practice of *Body Sourcing* that supports us to inquire within to the wisdom of the body.

I'm surprised when I develop a cold or flu, or when I injure myself, yet if I look closely it's usually evident where, when, and how I ignored the voice of my body when it was trying to get my attention. If I'd have listened, I could have taken appropriate steps to slow down, shift my diet or been more mindful of circumstances in order to avoid illness or injury.

Sensual Fitness

Sensual Fitness is different than physical fitness because it not only addresses the needs of the physical body; it includes the needs of the emotional and psychological/mental dimensions of our being, all the realms of our being. Together these three realms: physical, mental, and emotional comprise our spiritual realm.

 Sensual fitness means I strengthen my physical body and my practice of listening respectfully to the truth of what my whole self needs.

When I refer to spirituality, I'm using the definition of spirit as the one thread that weaves through all of life, connecting all life as one. At a microcosmic level, the union of each of the realms within us is a metaphor for the macrocosmic aspect of the union of all of creation.

The ability to sense, whether through conscious intention or by virtue of the intelligence that we embody, is how I define life. For instance, a tiger, like a human, can see, smell, and touch. A bean stalk doesn't have access to these senses as we know them, however, the ability to detect thirst, and thereby quench that thirst to encourage growth and the ability to sense light and grow toward that light is inherent in the life of that stalk. Studies have shown that plants can even pick up feelings of love or hate from the sounds and intentions of the people around them, thereby experiencing enhanced or diminished growth. So in this way, our senses support the life force within us, which is what connects us, and therefore are a spiritual dynamic of our existence. Sensual fitness, therefore, is essential for enhanced life experience.

Sensual fitness includes the practice of listening to your sensing awareness and choosing activities that respect and honor that sensual knowing. Sensual fitness can be anything that involves your physical body and your spiritual being. I'm a firm believer and example of someone who keeps my physical body fit without compromising my spiritual needs. I choose my exercise based on what feeds me on both levels. There's no one right choice. What's important is that you listen inwardly, identify what's true for you as a unique and powerful woman, and make the right choice for you in each moment. Consistent practice at listening makes it much easier to hear, identify, and choose. But we each have to start somewhere, and at first it can be hard to honor your own truth, especially if it's contrary to everything you've learned and what others approve of.

Here are a few examples from my own life:

My husband is a cycling fanatic and I love bike riding with him. His first choice is road biking for the thrill of the speed and momentum that he can sustain. At a sensual level he's exhilarated through his entire physical body and this gives him an experience of spiritual ecstasy. For him, road biking is a sensual fitness activity. I, on the other hand, cannot stand the sensation in my body that happens when cars go racing by. It detracts from my enjoyment. Instead of being exhilarated I feel scared which isn't pleasurable for me. I prefer mountain biking where I can sense my body physically working and my equilibrium being challenged by the unpredictable terrain while enjoying the beauty of nature around me that my other senses adore. This is a fantastic sensual fitness practice for me.

Other sensual fitness practices that I love are yoga, explorative dance, Vividance, Nia, running on the beach, tai chi, qi gong, pranayama, and other breathing practices. However, to stay true to my sensual fitness practice, I choose which I will do each day and in each moment of my practice based on what my body and soul are asking for in that moment, instead of relying on a set routine or exercise prescription. As a result, my practice is a new and exciting original recipe that I discover every day for the first time.

If you are in the habit of an exercise routine that never changes or requires a teacher or class setting, I encourage you to start getting creative with your work out to make it a simultaneous *work in*. If this is difficult to even imagine, start small. Devote a brief portion of your allotted exercise time to something completely spontaneous that requires you to check in and be in the moment with what your body and soul desire.

Nature Connection

"If you have ever let your hands caress the slow, smooth curves of water-worn boulders, you have been touched by the erotic, sensual, elemental power of Gaia." writes Julie McIntyre in *Sex and the Intelligence of the Heart: Nature, Intimacy, and Sexual Energy.*

The blessed communion with nature that is available to you when you're able to intimately connect inwardly is a source of peace and bliss that is profoundly nourishing. The world of nature is constantly dancing a parade of sensual abundance, engaging us with her beauty and aliveness, tantalizing our senses, and mirroring our lush wisdom. "Nature is the most profound expression of unconditional love," says eco-therapy guru Michael Cohen. "Everything is re-used and recycled, nothing is rejected by it."

Michael teaches us that there is a magical web of life that connects all of creation, including you. In this web, the web strings extend back and forth between all living creatures and things. The sooner and more vividly you're able to acknowledge these web strings, the more inspired you'll be and able to live in harmony with and in service of the radiant natural world that gives you your life.

Savoring nature instead of saving nature is an important key to living more in our Sensual Power. When we sensually savor her blessings, we're more likely to act on her behalf in the understanding that we are one with her and therefore acting on our own behalf at the same time. When we're engaged in saving nature, we're still objectifying her, and this is the essence of the problem that our planet is facing. Julie McIntyre writes, "There is a direct relationship between our beliefs, values, and behaviors about sex, sexuality, and intimacy and our beliefs, values, and behaviors toward and about the environment and Earth." Objectifying, destroying, and dominating the natural world all have repercussions on the well-being of our own inner nature.

 **Choose to *savor* nature instead of *save* her.
Move from objectification to oneness.**

Flirting with Nature, one of the Vividly Woman practices, awakens us to the reciprocal flirtation that is always available to us, just waiting to be paid attention to and honored, when we savor nature's beauty and wisdom, and see ourselves in her mirror.

Flirting with Nature

I step into the forest not knowing how thirsty my eyes are for green. I am instantly drenched by her fountain of flora. Many months in the dry heat of Mexico have left me parched and ready for the moisture of this succulent land. I fondle the moss; I rub the leafy soil in my palms and smell its wealth. I cuddle a long straight fir against my pounding heart, pressing my flesh against her marrow to amplify my inner pulsing. I want to touch it all with my eyes, and I want to listen with my whole body. I want to be re-hydrated from the inside out and pour out laughter.

The smooth body of a leaf slides between my fingers. Rough tree bark confuses the padding of my palms. Patches of sky reach through the canopy and beg for attention. Whimsical stems with bell-like blooms flank her corridor urging me onward. I feel oozed through this trail of native witness.

I allow my senses to be awoken amorously this way and I am ecstatically enchanted. I blend easily with my surroundings. I can't help merging with the space that cradles me so effortlessly. Is it me flirting with her, or is she shamelessly flirting with me? I don't know which is which, similar to the chicken or the egg. Who cares anyway? I am being lustfully courted by this delicious place. I am inviting her to nibble at my ears, lullaby me sweetly, and shower me with romantic gifts, everything wrapped from head to toe in gloriously gorgeous greenness. There is no mistaking the sudden arousal of my body to her affections.

Almost without thinking I bashfully surrender to her seduction. I press my toes into her soil rich darkness, feel the coolness of her must, and the freshness of the moment as we awaken in each other's presence. We have given ourselves to each other, honored one another and all of creation in our union, recognizing our infinite ancestral familiarity. We are lovers, coniferous and sublime.

> *Flirting with Nature Practice*
>
> 1. When you walk this month, indoors and out, start to consciously connect to all the natural life around you. Send out *web strings* of connection from your heart to all the nature surrounding you. The trees, bushes, flowers, houseplants, pets, and sky etc. are longing to connect with you. Especially if you live or spend most of your time in the city, start to pay attention to the token expressions of nature in your midst. Send out your *web strings* and receive theirs. This is how we step into the web of life consciousness and open to the two-way dialogue that's taking place all the time between ourselves and what David Abrams coined "the more than human world."
> 2. Take time to *sensually* connect with nature. Smell, listen, watch, taste, and touch the beauty of the natural world and experience her sensing you back. Discover what it means to flirt with nature.

Sensual Power

As I mentioned in Chapter 1 when describing the feminine centers of power, power is something that we all have. It gets expressed uniquely by each of us, but it's something we each have access to and having it isn't nearly as challenging as feeling comfortable with it.

Sensual Power is one of those things that we've been led to believe is taboo in our culture. We get a really confusing message because in the media we see women portrayed as sexy, exciting and exuberant, yet in the worlds of politics, high finance, and education, women are portrayed, and often present themselves in a more conservative way. Which is the right image of a powerful woman? Is it one or the other, or is it both? Maybe we just need to compartmentalize our lives and live our sensually alive self at home after work hours but put on our masculine linear demeanor when we head out to work. Sounds like a recipe for schizophrenia to me!

And even if we could live like that, many women get home and have children to mind and meals to put on the table. They aren't feeling they have time or space to ooze and linger over the things that arouse their senses.

I believe that women's sanity and well-being depend on our living congruently and true to our authentic self in all areas of our lives. That's how we can be most effective and productive.

But how can we be true to ourselves while still getting the job done?

This is where the masculine and the feminine come into play, and because we all have both inside us, we just need to know how to Harness and Express them when needed.

Sensual Power and sensuality have both masculine and feminine expressions, meaning that when you go to work and need to engage your masculine, linear, goal-oriented self. you don't have to sacrifice your Sensual Power. You just have to know how the masculine plays within you and how to use the masculine gifts of harnessing and containment (we cover this in Chapter 8—Harness) to actually grow your Sensual Power and embody it effectively for the situation.

My early years of hiking and backpacking often saw me and my avid outdoorsman boyfriend, Manuel, out in the backcountry roughing it for a few days at a time. Nature called and we both loved to gear up and get out into the wild where there were no sounds but the birds, the creaking of the tall trees and the waterfalls we passed along the way.

These outings remain blessed memories and formative experiences in my evolving love and appreciation for nature. However, I began to realize that Manuel always had a persistent striving to get us somewhere as fast as possible. His masculine sensual way was usually directing, focusing, and driving the activity. I, on the other hand, preferred to wander and daydream my way, communing with the scents and textures at every turn. My feminine sensual way prioritized exploration, creativity, and expansiveness. Sometimes our differing ways would result in an undercurrent of conflict between us. He was more about where we needed to get to, and I was more about where we already were.

Years later, when I happened to start going on outings with a small circle of women friends, I noticed how profoundly different it was. We planned shorter distances whether hiking, biking or kayaking, and always had time and space to "stop and smell the flowers." It wasn't long before I was choosing the sister-accompanied outings over those with my lover.

In hindsight, I get why with Manuel we had to get where we were going. Darkness would eventually come and we needed to have covered the distance we intended in order to reach our desired location, which was what brought us there in the first place. I know this approach is not better or worse, just different. The masculine is different than the feminine. And the reality is that they are always dancing with each other within and around us and each has a distinctive Sensual Power that is important to what eco-therapist Joanna Macy calls "the great turning," the shift from the industrial growth society to a life-sustaining civilization.

The reality is also that in the very patriarchal world in which we live, driven predominantly by masculine values and mindsets, the masculine overshadows the values and sensibilities of the feminine. While both are absolutely necessary for life on this planet, a clear lack of balance is evident. But is it balance that we need to achieve, and which would bring peace, ease, and fulfillment? Or, is it more an understanding and appreciating of the attributes of each, and engaging each at appropriate times to enhance the other that would most serve us?

So many women who first come to a Vividly Woman circle start by sharing that they've lived almost exclusively in a masculine world in their work life for years. They feel cut off from their feminine aliveness and are starving for their true feminine nature. Many women think of their femininity as synonymous with their sensuality, and when they expand on what they most miss about themselves, it is their sensual self. Once in circle, and in the sacred and safe space of other sisters also craving more of their divine feminine juiciness, they start to melt away the hardened shell that formed to protect their softer essence.

It's natural to embody that shell-like boundary since most others are embodying it in our world. I personally have very little experience in corporate settings, but as the former stepmom of three teenage boys I can wholeheartedly relate. The feminine tends to shy inward from the overwhelming testosterone energetic. The nature of the feminine is soft, inward, compliant, flowing, and malleable. Without this quality in our world, there would be no meandering rivers, no melting snow, and no merging of the seasons. And without the sensual nature of the masculine that contains the water with riverbanks, the river would cease to flow. There would be no extreme temperatures to freeze water into snow, and there would be no distinct quality to the seasons.

The Sensual Power of each of these energies dancing together in no uncertain terms is what makes the world go round.

Sensation

So how do we resource Sensual Power? Sensual Power pertains to your sensing awareness of the world around you and the world within you. It is literally the felt Sense experience that lives in your body, and when resourced, gives you vital and truthful information in each moment. Valuing sensations of pleasure and giving ourselves permission to be motivated by them is an important element of our Sensual Power. Sensual pleasure can be anything from enjoying the fragrance of a rose, to savoring sensations of sexual arousal or as subtle as paying attention to the gentle nuances of what happens in your body when you feel sad or feel fear.

Sensations of sadness and fear are not typically considered pleasurable, and that's why we avoid them. However, it is precisely in the avoidance that we create pain and discomfort and rob ourselves of the potential of pleasure that is an important component of our Sensual Power. Chronic avoidance creates incongruence in our behavior and is ultimately disempowering. Incongruent behavior sends a confusing message out into the world, the antithesis of refined and effective leadership.

Sensual Power lives primarily in your pelvic area. This is the lowest of the three power centers that correspond to the three body weights, the heaviest and most energetically charged areas of the body. The pelvic and hip area that is the center of Sensual Power is the center that is the closest to the earth. It has the strongest relationship to Mother Earth, which is the source of our physical body, and it has a profound resonance with the mothering instinct and the Mother Goddess archetype.

Anatomically this area also houses the sexual organs that initiate conception, the womb where embryonic life nurtures and grows, as well as the domain of so much sexual pleasure, so it's not hard to understand why this area would be strongly associated with Sensual Power.

> ### *Sense Your Sensual Power Practice*
>
> Take a moment now if you would, and please place one or both of your palms on your belly and take a few nice deep breaths. As you inhale, fill up your belly just like a balloon. As you exhale, let it empty so that your belly moves back toward your spine, in and out, riding the wave of your breath. Give your belly the fullest permission to be nice and round and full on each inhalation.
>
> This place, this womb, this vessel within you, houses all your sexual organs. These organs, whether you have them physically or energetically, are responsible for your creative potential in the world. Even if they've been removed, or you never had them to begin with, they are still with you energetically. I never had fully formed ovaries, and yet the Sensual Power that lives within me is strong and vital.

Pleasure

Not only are our sexual organs responsible for procreation, they are also responsible for your sexual pleasure. Have you ever considered how much your pleasure motivates you?

Can you imagine a life without pleasure? Is there anything you crave more than pleasure itself? It's clear to me that pleasure motivates. What if we gave ourselves the fullest permission to be motivated by pleasure? What mountains do you think we could move?

I believe there is enough power in just one of the Sensual Power centers of any one woman on this planet to do all the work that ten women need to get done in a week. That's a lot of stuff right? When we get comfortable with our Sensual Power, we become that powerful person that others are in awe of. You've seen it in other women and told yourself either that you could be that woman if you had umpteen conditions in place, or you have told yourself that you'll never be that woman because you don't have *that kind* of power. When you shift your perspective to embrace the truth that you don't need more power, both of the above excuses become unfounded and obsolete.

So how is it that we've allowed ourselves to shut down our very own Sensual Power centers? The answer to that question is different for each one of us.

Janet shared her story at Sacred Sensual Splendor, the Vividly Woman Mexico retreat that we've nicknamed the "Vividly Woman Honeymoon." She had four kids in five years, and couldn't stand the thought of getting pregnant again, so she completely shut down to her husband.

Janet didn't feel that she had the right to decide when and if she wanted to be sexual. So instead, she cut off her sexual aliveness so that her husband wouldn't be attracted to her. Does that sound familiar? Do you ever shut down your sensual/Shakti energy because it might threaten, attract or distract, others?

Another of my Vividly Woman Sisters, Carol, told the story of how as a girl she loved to ride horses, a passion that remains with her as an adult. Now as a mother of three she still rides, owns, and looks after several of her own horses.

At around age ten she was asked to write a story in her English class. She wrote about an exciting experience she had when she rode bareback, galloping in blissful union with her mare. A physical sensation of pleasure would overtake her that was profoundly pleasing but she was oblivious as to why this caused her so much enjoyment. Her teacher had the students read their stories aloud to the class. When Carol read her story, it caused embarrassment in the male teacher who recognized this young girl's sensual awakening and arousal in response to the thrusting motions against her vulva as she rode.

There was some awkwardness after the story was read that affected Carol, making her feel inappropriate and shameful. This experience wove itself into her burgeoning womanhood and ultimately became part of the foundation of her sensual and sexual beliefs about herself and the world, disabling her fullest potential for Sensual Power.

Sensuality

Literally, sensuality means being pleasing to the senses. That means that when you are being sensual you are pleasing your senses like enjoying the taste of a cupcake or watching a beautiful sunset, slithering naked on a cashmere blanket, listening to your favorite opera or smelling the fragrance of a blossoming rose. This act of pleasing your five senses gives you access to your sensuality. Since pleasure is extremely motivating, captivating, and engaging, your senses have a tremendous power to determine your actions or lack of them.

I'm motivated to buy certain ingredients that will enhance the taste of the food I prepare, and I tend to take a specific route when going on my morning run because I like what I get to look at. If you are a sensual person you will refer to your senses often, and though you may not know it, you are actually deferring not to the outside stimuli, but to the corresponding sensation within you that is a response to that outer stimuli.

Being embodied means bringing those body sensations into your awareness so that you're in touch with how the world around you is affecting the world within you. With this awareness you can make choices motivated not by the cupcake, but by your own potential for pleasure that lives inside of you in response to it, including the sensations that arise as your crave it. When you claim that, you are living your Sensual Power, owning the power for yourself instead of giving it away to the cupcake!

Craving

Craving is an important topic in the Vividly Woman Embodied Leader Training. We focus on it because craving has enormous potential to either derail us or empower us. It's like a secret weapon that we can use for inner peace or inner battle.

Craving is commonly judged as wrong and bad. "You shouldn't crave what you don't have, you shouldn't be needy or covet things." But think about it, craving arouses you. It gets the blood to your vulva, makes your nipples erect, inspires you to lust and strive. In and of itself, the aliveness of the body that is a result of craving is very delicious, and we all want more of that.

Perhaps it's not the craving, but the attachment to the item of our craving that's the problem. Anytime we attach to something outside of ourselves as the answer to our suffering, we create more suffering. Instead, what it's essential to realize is that we can only crave what we already know and embody. For instance, we can't crave chocolate unless we already know the body and mood enhancing effects of chocolate. If you've ever consumed chocolate, the experience of chocolate, including the satisfaction and pleasure it gives you, is already inside of you. Instead of looking outside, we need to be guided by our cravings to look inside. Celebrate the arousal that craving inspires, and refer within to satisfy it!

 . . . and then I understood with my whole being this line from a Rumi poem, "The longing is the answer."

I love this wisdom channeled by *Law of Attraction* authors Esther and Jerry Hicks from a group of entities called Abraham, because it captures the essence of craving, "You intended to come forth into the physical realm of contrast to define what is wanted. To connect with the energy that creates worlds, and to flow it toward your objects of attention. Not because the objects of attention are important, but because the act of flowing is essential to life."

I first discovered the art of craving after a tumultuous breakup. Have you ever experienced a loss so painful you just wanted to curl up and hide? That's where I was. Devastated, rejected, and terrified to be on my own, I watched as my whole body contracted around the hurt, clamping my heart shut. This body reaction was very familiar to me. It reminded me of what occurred when my father died suddenly twenty-five years earlier. In my shock and grief I'd retracted inward and had literally spent the next twenty-five years dancing my heart open. My father's sudden death had in fact catalyzed me finding dance as a healing path.

Now, twenty-five years later I could sense at a visceral level this same body reaction taking place. I was clear that I wasn't willing to let that happen again. I had to find a way to open my body, to surrender and melt my heart.

Living and working in a small beach town on the Pacific coast of Mexico, by day I taught yoga and dance and worked as a massage therapist. At night, I'd go out onto the beach and lie on my Mexican blanket and gaze up into the infinite night sky. I knew that if I was going to find God anywhere it was here under the stars. As I lay there I would practice surrendering my body's weight onto the earth in an attempt to release the tightening around my heart. I sensed, and intuitively knew, that the opening I craved already lived inside me. I had achieved it through years of dance, bodywork, therapy, and tender lovemaking. I could taste it so it must be inside me. The place for me to resource it from then was also within me. I realized that everything I craved was also already inside me in this very same way, and then I understood with my whole being this line from a Rumi poem, "The longing is the answer." That to long for God means that you already have God, and the more you long, the more you'll have the essence of what you ache for, as long as you look inside for it.

Sensual Craving

Sensual craving expresses itself as desire for sensual fulfillment which includes the desire for pleasure of all the five senses as well as the myriad sensing awarenesses that are available to the body. The sexual sense, known as desire or libido, is one of these.

Sensual craving brings a dimension of aliveness and vividness to a woman's life that is absent when she cuts herself off from the richness of her senses. A woman who's in touch with and honoring her senses is an attractive force that inspires opening and arousal in the people around her. This can have great benefits both personally and professionally. With sensual craving we learn to appreciate the blessing of the body's ability to sizzle with delight, and to harness that throbbing aliveness for all our endeavors and not just sexual activity.

The Light and Shadow of Sensual Power

Each of the power centers has both a light and shadow expression. Our culture has used the shadow expression of each of our power centers to cast our power as weakness, causing us to suppress it and undermine the potential embodied in its light expression, throwing out the baby with the bath water essentially.

The light expression of Sensual Power is a woman's abundant right and wealth of sensual aliveness that she can access and use to express her connection to what gives her pleasure, as a source of well-being. When a woman is in the light aspect of her Sensual Power, she resources her pleasure and uses it appropriately and responsibly.

A shadow expression of Sensual Power is apparent when a woman uses her sensuality to win emotional love, finds her self-worth predominantly in her sexuality or ability to attract a lover, flirts with people who are not available, dresses out of sync with her environment or in such a way as to flaunt sexuality where inappropriate, e.g. a mini skirt on a construction site. These are examples of leaking sexual energy instead of a mature harnessing and honoring of its tremendous allure and power.

Body Image

A woman's body image, her beliefs about the way her body looks, is profoundly linked to her sense of pride or shame about herself and self-worth. Marcia Hutchison writes in her book *Transforming Body Image*, "In a woman, body esteem and self esteem are married to one another."

If you carry shame about your sexuality or believe that there is something dirty or shameful about your sexual nature, it will undoubtedly show up in how you relate to your body and how you think your body looks. Your body image is not the truth about your body, rather it is the way you perceive your body looks and is often distorted and out of touch with reality. This could result in excessively needing your body to conform to societal standards of beauty, completely obliterating your sexual expression, masking it with the way you dress, or overstating it.

 Sensual Power guides us to listen inwardly to sensation instead of looking outwardly to the mirror for what's real.

Women are profoundly identified with the way we think our body looks and especially whether it conforms to our culture's standards of beauty. On top of that exaggerated need for fitting in, we also have a chronic inability to look at and see our body accurately. Our minds distort reality because of the beliefs, judgments, and shame that we carry.

Sensual Power gives you the ability to connect with your body from the inside instead of relying on a mirror. It's the difference between the experience of your body and the experience of what your body looks like. If you're always motivated to exercise because of the way you look in the mirror, you will use your body like a machine. If, on the other hand, you're devoted to your health and well-being, you will inhabit your body like a temple, listening to what you sense on the inside, and be guided and motivated by that. If you're used to chronically avoiding what's going on inside of you because it's uncomfortable to look at the truth, listening inwardly will be a foreign experience. The avoidance of inner truth creates *shadow,* and that causes us to suffer.

Shadow

Shadow is a term coined by Carl Jung that refers to aspects, memories or characteristics that we suppress in order to avoid pain. Unfortunately, in their suppression they wield enormous power and chip away at our self-esteem and self-worth, manifesting as drama, chaos, and unhealthy patterns of relating. The good news about shadow is that it's also the bearer of gifts. "… the shadow, in seeking the light of consciousness is the driver of growth," write Connie Zweig and Steve Wolf in their book *Romancing the Shadow*, "So inherent in the shadow is the potential for growth that we may realize if we have the courage to touch those dark painful places."

Shadow is not wrong, it's an aspect of every person on this planet, and your ability to confront it, to embrace it, and learn from it will determine how whole a woman you can be. In one of the Vividly Woman experiential initiations, each woman is invited to spend time with her deepest, darkest shadow issues, and then to actually make a voluntary choice to return to the land of shadow, recognizing its value to heal, transform, and expand her consciousness into the mature woman she is ready to be.

One of my greatest shadow teachers was a dance student of mine who shared with me, after a particularly emotionally moving dance class, how challenging it was to allow herself to feel and sense her body. She'd been conceived during a violent rape and had spent her life despising herself and her body because of the pain her mother had endured during her conception, and for being a living reminder of the horror of that experience. Her very physical existence was relegated to the realm of shadow. When she was ready to go deeper into the healing potential of dance, she took part in a shamanic trance dance ritual I was facilitating that literally had her meeting her shadow head on. Though she was terrified of what she might find there, the dance turned out to be a re-birth. Her courage to go into the darkness of her greatest fear, actually allowed her to experience the light of her conception and the blessed being she truly is. She stopped hating herself once and for all. This example stands out for me, but I have literally facilitated this dance ritual for thousands of individuals, in small and large groups, and the transformation stories have been many.

Bringing shadow into the light of consciousness can be profoundly liberating. One of my Vividly Woman sisters, Amy habitually shied away from her shadow, unable to confront the fears and pain she had long suppressed. "In the past, my shadow was a very scary and lonely place to be, but I had perfected ways of avoiding it by drowning it out with food, readily offering myself to fix other people's problems or calling friends to gossip. Now for the first time in my life, I did nothing. I simply stayed with it. Although it was almost unbearable at first, I actually began to invite it, and thus began an intricate dance. Seven months and several graceful waltzes, passionate tangos, and grueling river dances later, I've picked up a few invaluable lessons from dancing with my shadow:

1. My shadow will not kill me! In fact, it's my greatest teacher. Even though there are things that are hard to face about myself, I now choose to embrace every part of me in order to take action and change what doesn't work. Inviting the dance with my dark side is the only way to the light.
2. The power of avoidance is all engulfing! When I avoid handling a situation, emotion, or belief it just grows like a weed. Without restraint, it will eventually take over and poison everything.
3. I can't depend on anyone else (including my husband and children) to bring me happiness; make me feel worthy, sensual, or important; or even 'fix' any given situation. First of all, there is nothing to 'fix.' Things simply are, and it's all about how I choose to perceive them. The meaning I attribute to any situation is up to me, which means I am solely responsible for my emotions and—this was a real shocker when it hit

me—ultimately, my life! Yes, I have played the MAIN role in creating everything I don't like in my life . . . right now specifically my finances, weight, and non-existent screenwriting career.

4. Even though I've played the main role in creating it all, I don't have to beat myself up about it. In fact, one of my juiciest and most recent nuggets of wisdom is that guilt and shame are toxic emotions that I've subconsciously used to keep myself stuck in negative behaviors. The upside is that I have the power to change whatever I don't like. I've also manifested everything I love about my life!

5. Ever since I've let up on judging myself, keeping myself lodged in the guilt and shame, I've finally been able to hear some major subconscious beliefs that have held me back for so long: "I don't deserve." "I am not important enough." "My voice doesn't matter."

6. Having a shadow means that you're human. There's no pressure to pretend I have it all figured out. I don't, and probably never will! But I do know that the dance is a journey, and along the way I've picked up the most valuable gift of all: Faith. I had no idea that accepting my shadow as an intimate dance partner would lead to my greatest enlightenment. Just as I have no idea how I'm going to change the things that my shadow has now shed light on . . . but I have faith, and I know that it will all work out because I'm no longer afraid to share, exactly as I am, and let my voice be heard. Left palm up, right palm down (The Vividly Woman Mudra)."

Sexuality

Sensuality and sexuality are often confused and used interchangeably. They are related, though actually very different. I believe that the synonymous usage that they've experienced is a reflection of a patriarchal interpretation. Sensuality, being typically a more feminine quality, has been swallowed up in sexual context by a failure to understand it's essence in our patriarchal, fast moving, results oriented world.

Sensuality has become the foundation for my existence, rather than just my sex life.

Sensuality, being of the senses, has to do with our subtle and unique connection to life through our senses. Sexuality is all about the anatomical act of sex. Sexuality does not always include sensuality, though personal experience has shown me that the more sensually present I am, the more pleasurable the sex. Thus, when we tap into our Sensual Power during sex, we amplify our potential for energetic arousal and orgasmic pleasure. Because women are so sensually motivated, it stands to reason that honoring our sensuality will enhance sex and lovemaking.

In addition, the synonymous use of these two words would have us relegate our sensuality exclusively to the act of sex. The truth is that most of us spend less than one percent of our waking lives actually having sex. I want my life to be that juicy all the time, not just once in a while between the sheets or on the living room floor. I can enjoy more of the juiciness of life by engaging my sensuality more of the time, which allows me to claim that I am making love to life as a daily practice. With this, my sensuality has become the foundation for my existence, rather than just my sex life.

Sexual abuse is a huge topic that comes up in sacred woman's circles, and while the full breadth of this subject is beyond the scope of this book, it's important to touch on how it shows up in relationship to our Sensual Power. Please know that there are many wonderful teachers, therapists, and books devoted exclusively to this issue and I encourage you and all my Vividly Woman Sisters to resource these if a history of sexual abuse is part of your past. I've included a few in the resources at the back of this book.

Sexual Abuse and Sensual Power

I know a woman, Joy, who was sexually abused by her father until he died when she was sixteen. She hid the abuse for many years, comforting herself with food to hide her shame and the fear she felt as a child that someone would find out and blame her. She carried extra weight as protection against being perceived as sexual by other men so she wouldn't have to relive the enormous shame she embodied but kept at bay.

Sensual Power is de-stabilized by the history of abuse we carry. Whether a woman has been party to sexual molestation or got in the habit of saying yes to sex when she really felt no, and as a result became a master at splitting off (fragmenting her mind from her body in order to tolerate the experience and survive it) or harbors a profound fear of intimacy because of fear of rejection, Sensual Power will suffer and be suppressed. Each of the above scenarios causes the development of shadow material around our Sensual Power.

The journey home to your authentic power does necessitate you looking at the ways that your power was taken from you and the ways that you gave it away. One or both of these may be an aspect of a history of sexual abuse. If this is a part of your journey home (and it is for so many women because of sexual abuse and self-betrayal of their true sexual desires and preferences), touching the tender places of wounding within will be scary, especially at first. We've armored against sensing so that we won't feel the pain that abuse caused. When we start to venture inside to feel what we've taken enormous pains to avoid, it's like picking at a very sensitive scab. I hate to be the bearer of bad news, but the truth is that you will have to face some scary monsters in order to emerge into the light. The good news is that you are not alone on this journey, and the book you're reading is a testimony to the power of women supporting women as we each weave and dance our way home to reclaiming our sensual power. In Chapter 9—Express, you'll read about how you can learn to take back your power by saying no to another, in order to say yes to yourself.

Sensual Power at Work

Since Sensual Power is all about the body, and the health of it, it plays a profound role in your professional life. Without the health of the body, we are at a severe disadvantage when it comes to excelling at anything. Our careers and goals can tolerate brief periods of illness or imbalance but will begin to suffer if long-term disability or disease ensues.

In the patriarchal paradigm that so many of us grew up in, the message about our body was "Work like a dog if you want to get anywhere." There is a blatant disrespect of the body's needs and value placed on success at the expense of our health. The new paradigm encourages a new message "Honor your body and its authentic needs." to achieve a new version of success that values well-being, not accumulation of stuff and status.

This attitude of care vs. corrosion for our body, encourages personal integrity, and relates to the aspect of our business that is the product or service we offer. The degree to which we care for our body will be reflected in the quality of our offering. Whether you are an entrepreneur or a salaried employee, the integrity of your offering is essential for your success.

When *is* sensuality appropriate and what expression of sensuality is appropriate in the workplace? Can we even apply a generalized standard here? If sensuality expressed appropriately is Sensual Power, how can we measure and determine what is appropriate and where?

As mentioned above, power is authentic when we are at home and comfortable with it. It must be born of a true felt Sense embodiment rather than a reaction or protection. When our sensuality is an expression of a connection to our felt Sense connection to our internal world, it is contained and harnessed in such a way that inspires instead of threatens others. It sends a message of self-respect versus need for attention and attempt to solicit a reaction from others.

Relationship to the Textures

As you'll see in Chapters 5 and 6, Sensual Power relates primarily to the first two Vividly Woman textures, Sense and Ground. What this means is that on the spectrum of the textures, which are the planets in the Vividly Woman Solar System that constellate around the sun center where the three power centers reside, Sense and Ground most activate our sensual wisdom. Refer to the diagram at the back of this book to see this visually. Inquiry of these two textures in your life and how you relate to them will reveal your own sensual wisdom, bringing into conscious awareness the truth of your soul's longing and authentic resonance.

When you come into contact with deeply held parts of yourself that have been buried by years of living based on other people's needs and standards, you wake up to the true you and feel the relief of self-discovery. You suddenly become aware that you don't have to keep hiding who you are anymore or fit into others' expectations. As you sense your truth and as you ground within yourself and your body, you align with your Sensual Power.

Triple Goddess Archetype

The Triple Goddess archetype is used by many feminist-based spiritual groups and explored at length by historians and thought leaders including Carl Jung, Marija Gimbutas, and Robert Graves. It identifies the three stages in a woman's life, Maiden, Mother, and Crone, which correspond to the phases of the moon. These tie a woman's evolution to the natural rhythms in nature, and the realms of earth, underworld, and heavens, thus linking her to both the tangible and the intangible world of mystery.

The Sensual Power archetype is Mother. In this stage of life a woman is most profoundly absorbed in her role to provide fulfillment and stability and to experience her sexual aliveness as an expression of her mature womanhood. She also risks visiting and exploring her shadow lands to emerge more whole and more empowered.

Sensual Power Activist

Sensual Power in action to effect change is exemplified by the amazing Eve Ensler. Author, playwright, performer, and activist, Eve has birthed live productions, books, and global movements to raise awareness about gender-based violence and shift the global paradigm of women's relationships to their bodies. She is perhaps most known for her *Vagina Monologues*. My favorites are her one woman show, *The Good Body*, and her book, *Insecure at Last*. Her devoted activism is profoundly inspiring, and her work both embodies and encourages Sensual Power in women and girls. She is without a doubt one of the most dynamic women of our time.

Chapter 2 Summary: Sensual Power

~ Claiming and living our Sensual Power enables us to have good health, healthy sexuality, and sensual pleasure in everyday experiences.

~ Sensual fitness is different than physical fitness because it not only addresses the needs of the physical body; it includes the needs of the emotional, psychological/mental, and spiritual dimensions of your being.

~ The sensual aspects of both the masculine and the feminine are necessary and can complement each other if we consciously chose when and how to embody them.

~ The pelvic and hip area is where your Sensual Power is housed. It has a close relationship to the earth, which is the source of your physical body and has a profound resonance with the mothering instinct and the Mother Goddess archetype.

~ Since pleasure is extremely motivating, captivating, and engaging, your senses have a tremendous power to determine your actions or lack of them.

~ Being embodied means bringing your body sensations into your awareness so that you are in touch with how the world around you is affecting the world within you.

~ Sensual craving expresses itself as desire for sensual fulfillment which includes the desire for pleasure of all the five senses as well as the myriad sensing awarenesses that are available to the body.

~ Valuing sensations of pleasure and giving yourself permission to be motivated by them is an important element of our Sensual Power.

~ When a woman is in the light aspect of her Sensual Power, she resources her pleasure and uses it appropriately and responsibly. The shadow expression of Sensual Power can be a leaking of sexual energy instead of a mature harnessing and honoring of its tremendous allure and power.

~ Sensual Power gives you the ability to connect with your body from the inside instead of relying on a mirror. As you sense your truth and ground within yourself and your body, you are aligning with your Sensual Power.

~ The Sensual Power Goddess archetype is the Mother who risks visiting and exploring her shadow lands to emerge into a mature aspect of her womanhood.

**To arouse your embodied power,
visit our "Sensual Power" stimulators at**

www.VividlyWoman.com

> *"Our satisfaction in life comes from not pushing away the grief, but in feeling so moved and filled and permeated by it that we come to the center of all life".*
> ~Christine Caldwell

CHAPTER 3

Emotional Power

Mastering the Rich World of Your Emotions

Emotion: a feeling and the subjective experience of it

Emotional Power: Freedom to feel and mastery of choice of when and how to express those feelings

We've looked at Sensual Power and started the journey to reclaim our body as our temple. Some of that began to touch on what's stirring inside that not only has to do with physical sensation, but is also intimately interwoven with what we know as our feelings and emotions. Now, we'll cross the bridge from the Sensual to the Emotional to continue the adventure in pursuit of our inner power.

The words emotion and power don't often appear in the same sentence. In fact, emotions have long been used as a dirty word, something to avoid at all costs, while power is a long sought after commodity that people literally kill for.

Power is considered to be a natural quality of the masculine, and coincidentally, emotions are relegated to the world of the feminine. While women are thought to be overly emotional, we're discouraged from bringing that trait into professional settings, and many personal and family environments discourage it as well. As activist/author Eve Ensler writes in her memoir *In the Body of the World*, *"We have been trained to believe this bifurcation of heart and head is necessary, something that will protect us, that embedded in this detachment is some magical shield…"*

We've been taught that emotions make us weak, but if that were true, the empathy and love we feel for our loved ones that motivate us to care for and nurture them would be a detrimental thing. How can the very recipe that grows children into healthy adults be a detriment to our collective society?

Our emotions are a wellspring of potential for depth and intimacy. When you shut them down in one area of your life, you contract them in every area.

In the Vividly Woman Embodied Leader Training, emotions are one of the three dimensions of feminine power, along with Sensual and Intuitive Power, that we can resource for our well-being and authentic aliveness. The sad reality however is that in response to learning that emotions are disruptive, inappropriate and make us weak and vulnerable, women have profoundly denied our inner emotional landscape leaving us very shut down and out of touch with what is actually a rich and abundant natural inner resource.

At Vividly Woman, we define Emotional Power as a combination of your freedom to feel the truth of your feelings, and your ability to harness those feelings so that you're a master of them and they expand you instead of consume you. Giving yourself the freedom to indulge in your emotions without dumping them on others is essential for women because we do feel so passionately. Making time for regular emotional cleansing helps you prevent the build up of toxic emotional waste within you and making it anyone else's problem.

Emotions that are suppressed end up causing pollution in your body. You feel emotionally bloated and develop symptoms that are often difficult to trace back to the original offending substance/experience. But when you give your emotions the space to be felt, encouraging the enzymatic action of awareness, the undigested matter can move through you and be let go.

Expression, Suppression, and Digestion

The expression of emotions can take so many different forms. Besides talking about the emotions, delving into their story, which we'll look at more below, emotions find fulfilling expression in creative endeavors. Visual arts like drawing, painting, and sculpture. Expressive arts like dance and singing, and the healing arts like massage and energy work, can all bring enormous emotional relief and meaning. Find ways to channel your emotions as a way to express what's current on a regular basis. Just as you eliminate digestive waste and toxins on a daily basis, express emotional waste and toxins on a daily basis as well.

Choosing your expressive outlet responsibly is essential, and remembering that no one is obligated to witness your emotional expression, or has the right to demand that you be a witness to theirs. Emotions are an intimate inner experience, that shouldn't be used and wielded to evoke response from others. This abuse of emotional expression only comes around to haunt us, as we have to sit with our lack of integrity. I used to fake crying with my ex-husband to try and win his empathy and attention. It was also a strategy I used to impress upon him how much he was causing me to suffer, how wrong he was, and how right I was. Did it ever actually work? Maybe at first, but not only did he catch on, I still had to be with the lack of integrity within myself, and the reality that I was using my emotions to manipulate him.

Emotions that go unexpressed and are consistently denied become disease in the psyche and/or the body. I remember a teacher once telling me that if the body doesn't develop symptoms of repressed emotions, the mind will become unstable, eventually causing mental/psychological illness. Perhaps this is why depression has become so prevalent in our culture, along with panic attacks and states of anxiety.

Suppressed emotions and the life stories that generate them become shadow material that when unidentified as such can cause one's life to self-destruct, slowly or abruptly. Either way, whatever gets persistently relegated to the dark hidden corners will pop up in another nasty form and ultimately cause greater suffering and damage than the original emotions.

 Permission to feel deeply facilitates a woman's tender connection to self and others that encourages more fulfilling intimacy.

A woman who lives a life of routine emotional suppression is shutting off the tap on a wellspring of potential pleasure. Her gift of deep feeling can facilitate her tender connection to others, and that connection allows for a deeper, more fulfilling intimacy. This intimacy encourages women to produce a hormone called oxytocin. Oxytocin is a powerful hormone that is mostly known for making its appearance after a woman gives birth. The flooding of this elixir gives the new mother a euphoric feeling that allows her to largely forget, somatically and mentally, the pain she endured through labor. In our everyday life, oxytocin and the hormone serotonin encourage a feeling of well being. Both hormones get secreted in a woman's brain when she engages in intimate, authentic verbal sharing, the kind we do in circle as a regular part of the Vividly Woman training.

Emotions that are suppressed end up causing pollution in your body. However, expression can be equally as damaging if not done consciously and responsibly.

We always have the choice to impose our emotional process on others. This is like vomiting in public and expecting other people to clean up our mess. Sometimes our need to express emotions is an attempt to not feel them. We believe that we can somehow avoid the pain or discomfort of the emotion by directing its expression at someone else. Unfortunately, though there may be a temporary sense of relief, very temporary in fact, our conscience will come back to bite us because we know at a deeper level whatever gets expressed in outward emotion is inner turmoil that can only ultimately be resolved between self and self.

Emotions do need to be literally swallowed, taken in and felt, in order to be resolved. Suppressed emotions are swallowed emotions that are not felt and pollute our system, like undigested food. Food, as we know, needs to be ingested, release its nutrients, and be let go of in elimination. But in the process of digestion, the food gets transformed from food to chyme to waste. Emotions are also alchemically altered when they are given the space to be felt and, we can expel the toxins in a safe and inoffensive way through conscious and responsible vehicles of self-expression.

 Whether you are blaming somebody else or blaming yourself, the outcome is the same; the emotions are unresolved, undigested, and become toxic.

If you are holding on to emotions without resolution, it's like undigested food matter that sits in your colon, making your life toxic. How do we inhibit the digestion of our emotions? Anytime we feel blame, we are preventing digestion from taking place. Blame is like plaque on the walls of the intestine that prevent absorption of important vitamins and minerals or in the case of emotions, awareness that can be applied to one's life so that we suffer less and enjoy life more. These nutrients are like our important life lessons. The nutrients of our emotional world are the wisdom we gain that support our consciousness raising. Blame causes you to become a victim, which causes suffering. Whether you are blaming somebody else or blaming yourself, the outcome is the same; the emotions are unresolved, undigested, and become toxins. Instead, responsibility, awareness of the gift, and the learning, leads to power. Whenever we are blaming we take away our own power and give it to the person or situation we're blaming.

My favorite example of this is from the book *Unplugging the Patriarchy* by Lucia Rene. The three main characters in this book set out to dismantle the patriarchal constructs that have plagued our civilization for centuries. Instead of believing that they are victims of the patriarchy, they take on the role of being the architects of the patriarchy, believing that in having created the system themselves in a past life, they are much better equipped to take it apart and diffuse its power.

Just like these three characters, we each need to take full responsibility for whatever occurs in our life. When we do; we can rise above it and move on. As long as we are in blame, we'll suffer and feel helpless or dis-abled.

Empathy and Emotional Craving

Both our profound capacity to feel empathy and the value we place on feelings of love and our need for it are characteristics of being a woman in her authentic aliveness. These are important aspects of your emotional power and deserve to be honored as such.

A woman's ability to feel empathy and to value that feeling can be a rich source of her power. We all know that women are endowed with great attention for the well-being of others. Maybe it's not that we feel empathy more, just that we value it more.

We witness and experience the pain of others around us all the time. Reading the news, listening to the radio, images on the television whether truth or fiction, trigger the deep well of compassion that we feel. Even when we are not directly involved, we still feel grief for the plight of others. Respecting the grieving process on a daily basis is a vital way to nurture your Emotional Power. The more we make peace with what causes us to feel pain, the more abundantly we'll enjoy the more comfortable and celebrated emotions like happiness, joy, and enthusiasm.

At the deepest point of our souls, what motivates us to live day after day is the craving for love. That is the ultimate motivator. Whether it's love of another human being or knowing we are genuinely loved by God, the craving for love is so strong that we can even betray our own authentic needs and truths in order to acquire it. Does that make emotional craving bad? No, it just reminds us that healthy craving is always about our inner sensation versus the acquiring of anything external to ourselves, including love of God. The longing for love, in and of itself, can be a healing balm for whatever is not loving in your life. The illusion that you are without love can be soothed by the yearning for love itself as long as you look inward instead of become attached to something or someone outside of you.

Harnessing and Witnessing

We've been taught for so long that it's not okay to feel our emotions strongly, it's no wonder we've become good at denying them. In truth, the problem isn't feeling our emotions; the problem is letting our head distract us from the true felt sensation of that emotion in our body.

Let me explain. Inappropriate emotional expression is a result of chronically escaping from the emotions in the body in favor of the perpetuating thoughts that justify them. Said more simply: a mild feeling can erupt into a tantrum if the mind gets hold of it and starts weaving a drama or story around the feeling, all used as a tactic not to feel.

Whenever you have a feeling, you have a corresponding body sensation. If you were to automatically refer to the sensations, instead of focusing on the thoughts, you'd be honoring the feelings, giving them the space to be acknowledged and felt, and the freedom to dissolve and subside as well.

When you go up to your head, and obsess in the thoughts, it's like pouring kerosene on a fire. It expands the feelings, instead of the life force energy that is your core essence, and leads to overt often exaggerated and inappropriate emotional expression. While emotional expression is healthy when it's an authentic, self-responsible release of body held trauma, it can also be used as a weapon of manipulation and abuse when fueled by destructive thoughts.

We'll explore more on emotional expression in Chapter 9—Express.

Whenever you acknowledge yourself having strong feelings, remind yourself that you always have the choice as to whether or not you express what you're feeling. By enrolling your witnessing consciousness, you're able to stand back and objectively experience the feelings, instead of being swept away by the feelings or your story about them and being at their mercy. The key is to first cultivate your witnessing awareness and know that you have this choice.

Not expressing your emotions doesn't mean that you don't feel them, just that you understand that you can actually process your feelings in a healthy way independent of their outward expression. As well, you also recognize that outward expression may actually be a strategy to feel less, instead of feel more.

One of the practices that we use to objectively witness and honor our feelings is called the *Mood Goddess Practice*. In this practice we stand back from the prevalent emotion and personify her as separate from us, allowing us to have an objective perception and relationship with the emotion while giving it its full opportunity to be acknowledged and honored. Here's an example of how one of our Vividly Woman Sisters, Amanda, used this practice when she was in profound despair:

"Tonight I feel such enormous sadness and I sense it in my heart. I just ended a relationship with a wonderful man. It had run its course and I've known that for a number of weeks.

My Mood Goddess is called Dragona. She has long black silky hair, green eyes, and is clothed in a grey velvet gown with dragonfly wings. She sits heartbroken on the rocks by the sea. Her tears fall gently into the crashing waves . . . the smell of the salt-water fills her nostrils. The rocks are sharp and cold, unforgiving as she balances herself above the shoreline. All she hears is the faint whistle of the wind as it circles her like an angry beast. The moon desperately tries to comfort her with its luminous beams but the clouds are unforgiving . . . the color of blueberries they cast their shadow upon her.

She is alone but not afraid. Inside her heart burns a warm flame, steady and strong. Above her races a shooting star in all its brilliance. She takes flight . . . gone like the wind.

I can't wait to see where she lands . . .

Even with this tremendous pain I feel such hope. I'm so happy I can use this practice to express and heal my emotions."

In her book *Why Buffalo Dance*, Susan Chernak McElroy mentions that the Ancient Greeks personified their feelings and moods into gods and goddesses. By doing this they honored the emotional energies present in their lives helping to make subconscious information conscious. We can do this as well and participate in and welcome the process of waking up while remaining present as a witness rather than a victim to circumstances.

> ### *Mood Goddess Practice*
>
> What is the prevalent mood in your life these days? It could be an emotional quality or an energetic presence that you can feel around you. Sense this presence or quality. If it had a taste what would it be, if it had a smell, a sound, a color, what would it be?
>
> Give it a Goddess identity. Give her a name so that you can recognize her and befriend her.
>
> Use the Questions below to begin the process of embodying your Mood Goddess.

What is the prevalent mood in your life these days?

Describe her as a Mood Goddess using your senses.

She tastes like:

She smells like:

She sounds like:

She looks like:

Her texture is:

The name of my Mood Goddess is:

Archetype

The Goddess archetype corresponding to our emotional power is the Maiden. We can all remember a time when we identified ourselves with the young girl who felt the freedom to feel and express her emotions freely without censorship. At some point in our evolution into adulthood we lost the innocence of our emotional spontaneity and authenticity in favor of what was socially acceptable and expected of us. Unfortunately, the need to be *appropriate* castrated our emotional aliveness in many ways, causing us to betray our emotional integrity and the essence of our inner Maiden.

Truth vs. Story

Being in your Emotional Power means getting real with yourself and being willing to drop the drama and the stories you weave in your head in favor of the truths that your body knows. So much of the mental emotional anguish we experience is self-inflicted suffering caused by perpetuating stories that keep us rooted in victim consciousness. When we're ready to face the truth and our responsibility for it, our tolerance for story becomes very minimal. We naturally begin to gravitate more quickly toward what brings relief vs. what makes us right.

 Facing the truth and our responsibility for it reduces our tolerance for story and the suffering story causes.

A couple of years ago I was facilitating dance and creative awakening at a large event in California. A gentleman came over to me during one of the breaks, wishing to purchase my DVD for his wife. It turns out I'd lived close to them so we began a conversation about the area and some mutual acquaintances.

It didn't take long before Mark shared with me that his relationship with his wife was very fragile and they were in discussion about separating. With three children at home, this was not an easy conversation and they'd been trying to avoid making any rash decisions. I could feel his pain and sorrow. I gathered that the desire to end their marriage was more her leaning than his. He seemed dispirited and sorrowful, despite the fact that he was at a very upbeat gathering surrounded by lots of loving people. His wife, it turns out, had sent him to this event, to see if it might help their marriage. I could feel the sadness and resigned attitude of one who feels unloved and skating on thin ice in partnership. From personal experience, I knew what that feels like, and I couldn't help feeling deep empathy for him.

A year later, when I was facilitating at the same event, in the same location, I had the occasion to meet Mark's wife Laura who was attending the event this time. Once again, I was informed about the status of their relationship, this time from her perspective, and her dissatisfaction with their connection.

Laura was curious about the Vividly Woman Training so we spoke about it a little. Toward the end of the week, once we'd gotten to spend a little more time getting to know each other and I understood more about their situation and her thoughts and feelings, I couldn't help saying to her, "If you're not ready to leave him, don't come to the Vividly Woman Training. I've seen too many women get real and finally pull the plug on life situations that are starving them, after they've been in sacred circle with sisters." It seemed like a radical statement to make at the time. Sure enough, Laura joined us in Mexico that February at Sacred Sensual Splendor. By August she informed me she was leaving the marriage, and, jokingly added, all because of me.

We both knew she was joking. But the reality is, when you stop playing at story telling, the truth looks you square in the face, and you can no longer deny what's really causing you pain and suffering and what needs to be done about it, even when it means turning your life upside down.

A simple illustration to me of the power of the body's truth vs. the mind's story became clear to me when I decided to take up playing tennis as an adult. I'd played as a child but apparently tennis is not like riding a bike! When I got out on the court with my very patient husband, it was all I could do to get my racket somewhere near the ball. Hitting it with the racket frame was an achievement I could claim by the end of our first very brief venture into playing tennis together.

The next time we went out to play together, after several failed attempts to get a volley going back and forth between us, I was even more pathetic that our first time out, Greg suggested that we each take our own ball and play against the wall next to the court. What a difference. Somehow, I was able to maintain a steady to and fro between my racquet and the wall, and even hit the ball with the strings. It was confusing to me why this was so, since I was standing much closer to the wall and had to move and react much more quickly than when I stood on the opposite side of the net from Greg and had lots of time to line myself up and get the ball back to him.

After practicing in this way for a while we went back to trying it across the net, but once again, I was hopeless.

What became apparent to me later is that when playing with the wall I had far less time to react. There was no time to think and plan, only to let my body take over and find its way, given the current circumstances that were quickly and constantly changing. This was a profound affirmation for me that the body knows and the mind, which is always interpreting and analyzing with its addiction to story, can often just get in the way.

Light and Shadow

The light aspect of emotions is our ability to be informed by our emotions and process them in a healthy way that unburdens and relieves suffering.

Our insight awareness, what we'll explore in the next chapter on Intuitive Power, can help us to access and identify emotions as information. In fact, for some people, intuitive information comes in the form of emotions, or feelings.

Typically a feeling will arise, a fear for instance, that indicates there is something inviting caution, even though the conscious mind doesn't have an explanation or reason for fearful feelings. In this instance, the fear tells the mind to be cautious, and the mind identifies that as intuitive awareness; information to be acknowledged and taken seriously. In this way, a feeling has inspired an intuitive attention, independent of circumstantial evidence. We call these gut feelings. They are actually a combination of a feeling and a sensation.

Repressing these gut feelings dampens your Emotional Power and your Intuitive Power. Like any muscle, the less you use it, the weaker it gets.

On the other hand, when you respect your feelings, approach them with curiosity and interest, they'll teach you an enormous amount about yourself and your perception of the world around you.

The shadow aspect of our emotions, as discussed above, is the use of emotions to manipulate or the tendency to overindulge in our feelings or avoid them, which ultimately results in being consumed by them. Instead of freeing us to have more life energy, we get bogged down, heavy and dark and we radiate those feelings outward in an unspoken communication about how we are being in relationship with our self.

 Having a shadow is not the problem; it's how or whether you tend to it.

If your relationship with yourself isn't so pretty, it's going to be less inspiring for others to want to engage in relationship with you. Having a shadow is not the problem; it's how or whether you tend to it. As Amy reminds us in the last chapter, "Having a shadow means that you're human." Attending to your shadow is a healthy regular activity that will allow you to drink from the well of your own wisdom instead of perpetually flailing about trying not to drown in your own suffering.

Emotional Power at Work

When does business not have to do with relationships? Our customers, suppliers, colleagues, and partners are people with whom we are constantly navigating relationship. The heart and soul of any business is about relationship, and all dealings ultimately come down to how we are relating.

And when do relationships not have to do with emotions? Whether personal or business, relationships have the potential to elicit emotional response or reactiveness. The power of mastery with our emotions can make or break a relationship, a business deal, a promotion, a job offer or partnership.

The ability to witness our emotions and willfully choose which to express and when, while still honoring what we choose to postpone expressing, is a skill and mastery that serves in business beyond measure. We are not so much talking about self-control, but more about self-awareness, integrity, and self-responsibility.

I began a business venture with an acquaintance once whose work I admired. I was excited to work together on a book and a whole series of offshoot products and programs to go with it. Every time we met at our appointed time, she would spend at least forty-five minutes sharing her cares and woes. It was emotionally exhausting to have to sit and listen. I just didn't have the time and space in my busy work schedule to have to be a party to her issues. It felt like a serious drain on my resources. For this reason, I came around to the decision that working together was not a fit for me. I gracefully and tactfully shared that our partnership was not working out for me and I would need to rescind my intention of partnership with her. It was disappointing for us both, but it felt like the most honest and self-caring thing I could do at the time.

The reason I chose not to work with her wasn't because I judged her for her issues, but because her lack of ability to choose the appropriateness of expressing them during our work together told me something important about her level of emotional maturity. This insight nudged me to wonder how reliable a partner she would be as we moved forward in our endeavors. I saw the potential for more drama and complications as we continued and I was clear that these were not qualities I wanted in my life or my business.

I believe that we are always being sized up in this way by those we want to do business with. Whether consciously or unconsciously, our mentors, prospective clients, and partners have their antennas detecting these cues and are making decisions about their involvement based on this information. In essence what this means is that we are always marketing ourselves and that our Emotional Power is closely linked to our marketing. So in summary, what this points to is that access to our Emotional Power, or lack of it, can make or break not just one business deal but possibly the viability and life of your business or job.

Emotional Power in Relationship to the Textures

Emotional Power corresponds to the third and fourth textures, Mobilize and Harness. As we'll see in each of these chapters, the meaning of the heart, and grounding in that meaning to create self-sustaining behaviors and systems, is a vitally empowering habit for becoming more energetically efficient and mature.

Emotional Power Activism

To be motivated by the power of love, and to let that be a driving force that makes you unstoppable has been modeled for us by a woman who will certainly be known for all of history. Mother Teresa, an Albanian born nun, was called to devote her life to the poor and the suffering. Through the missionary that she founded, she led thousands of others to serve, open heartedly and without compensation, those with AIDS/HIV, leprosy and tuberculosis. My favorite Mother Teresa quote is "I have found the paradox, that if you love until it hurts, there can be no more hurt, only more love".

Chapter 3 Summary: Emotional Power

~ Our emotions are a wellspring of potential for depth and intimacy. When you shut them down in one area of your life, you contract them in every area.

~ Emotions that are suppressed end up causing pollution in your body.

~ No one is obligated to witness your emotional expression or has the right to demand that you be a witness to theirs.

~ Whatever causes you to suffer because of the illusion that you are without love, can be soothed and attended to by the yearning for love itself as long as it motivates you to look inward instead of being dependent and attached to something outside of you.

~ Blame prevents self-awareness that can be applied to one's life, which would encourage us to suffer less and enjoy life more.

~ Witness consciousness facilitates Emotional Power.

~ Emotional expression can be used as a weapon of manipulation and abuse when fueled by destructive thoughts.

~ Not expressing your emotions doesn't mean that you don't feel them, just that you understand that you can actually process your feelings in a healthy way independent of their outward expression.

~ Outward expression may actually be a strategy to feel less instead of feeling more.

~ The Goddess archetype of Emotional Power is the Maiden and her authentic uncensored emotional landscape.

~ The ability to witness our emotions and willfully choose which to express and when, while still honoring what we choose to postpone expressing, is a skill and mastery that can serve us in business relationships.

**To arouse your embodied power,
visit our "Emotional Power" stimulators at**

www.VividlyWoman.com

"Once you awaken your intuition and get in the habit of listening to and acting on it, every decision in your life will become reflective of your inner truth".
~Gabriele Roth

CHAPTER 4

Intuitive Power

Dancing Your Higher-Self

Intuition: higher self-wisdom

Intuitive Power: the ability to decipher between higher self-truth vs. ego, and proceed in alignment with the former, intuition

Now that we've dabbled in the Sensual and Emotional realms, we're primed to explore the third aspect of our power, Intuitive Power. Honoring the wisdom of our body and our emotions gives us greater access to our intuition by encouraging our awareness of when it uses those as vehicles to speak to us.

When I was a little girl, around six or seven, my family spent weekends and summers in the Laurentian Mountains outside of Montreal. We had a beautiful log house that was comfortable and cozy right on Sixteen Island Lake. All the homes around this lake are only accessible by boat, or some, like ours could be accessed by a walking trail that circled the lake.

Some days when I felt the call of the wild, I would venture out on this walking trail all on my own. I'd pack a lunch, and set out on a walk-about around the lake. Each time, when I arrived at a stand of birch trees, I would turn around and head back to my safe little world of family and family friends. I have no idea now how far that trail took me, or what happened for me on those walks, but I distinctly remember those ritual outings by myself in nature.

These days, when I set out to walk, I have a few intentions. One intention is to move my body, another is to clear and ease my mind, and another is to soothe my heart. As a child, I couldn't have had any other conscious motivation other than to do something exciting on my own, and enjoy my own company. Even though I don't remember what happened on those walks, I sense that those were important times in the development of my intuition. The need to fit in, to be accepted, and to be loved were all suspended while it was just nature and me. All those other ego needs are exhausting for an adult, not to mention for a child.

Intuition is awareness and acknowledgement of higher self-truth. It's what we know but often ignore because it may be in contrast to what the ego wants. Learning to distinguish between these two voices: ego, from intuition, is a profound way to create more ease and less suffering.

 Ego isn't bad or wrong, but we do need to be able to distinguish its voice from that of our intuition.

Like power, as I discussed in Chapter 1, intuition is something we all have. Intuitive insights are constantly being offered to our conscious awareness. Our ego needs are what get in the way of us choosing to notice those awarenesses, acknowledge their existence, and be motivated to act on them. Ego isn't bad. It's a necessary part of our Self that allows us to function and strive, but we need to be able to identify what is running us in each moment. When we defer exclusively to ego, it's loud drone occludes the voice of intuition so that it becomes a bare whisper, and is almost completely drowned out. That's one of the characteristics of ego. It's not very sensitive to other possibilities. It gets attached easily and once it's attached, it struggles to hang on. That's why it's important to be able to consult with both ego and intuition, and to be able to distinguish between them to make wise and realistic choices.

I've chosen ego over intuition enough times, and witnessed the outcome, to now know that ignoring my intuitive wisdom is counter productive. It's important for each of us to become conscious of our own dance between ego and intuition. It's most helpful if you can recall times in your life when the outcome of a situation didn't meet your deepest needs. Can you look back and recall an intuitive nudge that you didn't pay attention to or an inner stirring that was tugging at your awareness but which you didn't heed?

Intuition can come in the form of doubts and hesitations, but these aren't necessarily an indication of what your course of action should be. If we wait to proceed only when we don't have second thoughts we may never actually step in to action. So, it's precisely when you are torn and there are multiple considerations, when it's especially important to notice which part of you is saying what, and why that is.

I notice that problems and inner struggle most arise when my ego is being heeded more than my intuition and my ego is shadowing my intuition to such an extent that I can't hear it with my mind. In this chapter we'll explore the relationship between Intuitive Power and the sensual body and

I'll guide you to discover the felt Sense experience of intuition vs. that of ego within your body temple so you can make body conscious choices.

One of the last times I blatantly ignored my intuition is a comical example of the lengths we go to in order to feed the ego at the expense of the soul. When a promoter approached me who was interested in helping me grow my business and my following, I was intrigued and cautious. As we chatted, on multiple occasions, Fiona, a well-spoken, seemingly well-connected professional in her field, spouted idea after idea and names of well-known celebrities and authors whom she felt certain would endorse my work and make it easy to expand Vividly Woman into a household brand. To say I was excited is putting it mildly. Ecstatic and overwhelmed was more like it. I had finally made it. Somebody who could really help Vividly Woman and me. At last I would cash in on all my hours and hours of devoted work and service. I would be featured in Oprah Magazine, be a guest on the Bill Maher show, and appear at a private Stevie Nicks gathering. I felt like I'd struck the jackpot. I'd been discovered, my fairy goddess mother had dropped from the heavens and I was ready!

Despite all the glitter and excitement she promised, during the course of these conversations, something inside me felt uncomfortable. I hadn't hired Fiona yet, and we hadn't even discussed her fee, but already I was sensing a warm nervousness in my belly and chest, and a feeling of not really trusting her. I spoke to my husband about this woman who had suddenly appeared in my life, and he, too, was suspicious. After looking at her website, we began an online search to determine if she was one of America's known scam artists. Reviewing a resume and list of referrals is one thing, but when you're researching to see if she has a history of scamming, you've got to wonder what part of "run the other way Leela" isn't getting through to you.

As time went by, and we couldn't find anything on her to suggest we be concerned, there was still always a nagging feeling inside me. Now, not only was she promising things that were beyond my wildest dreams, her way of relating started to really turn me off. "Straighten up, be a man," she'd say to me when I was wishy-washy around a certain issue concerning business. Be a man? Statements like this were the antithesis of everything I teach and yet were still not enough to pull the plug on our newly kindled working relationship.

The messages from my body and my emotions were strong enough to make me experience caution. However, six months and several thousands of dollars later, I was asking myself "What about those hints was I not getting that had me completely ignore the signs and signals and venture forward with her anyway?" Clearly, the rewards that my ego imagined possible were more tempting than my need for and devotion to inner peace and integrity with myself. I wouldn't say there was absolutely no benefit to our working together, but the corrosion to my self-trust was the worst casualty. I knew there was something off, yet I chose not to listen. This kind of repeated blindness sends a message to your intuition that you don't trust it, and thus its voice becomes less and less audible in favor of the ego's seductions.

Witness Consciousness

Intuitive Power gives us the ability to witness, objectively, what is taking place within us on all levels; sensually, emotionally, mentally, and spiritually. It's the bird's eye view to be able to see the larger perspective and the details at the same time, with the ability to maintain an objective perspective. The Goddess archetype of Intuitive Power is the Crone: the wise elder who has lived and learned.

The mind, responsible for our mental faculties, is an essential aspect of Intuitive Power because it allows us to cultivate witness presence. The mind is supported by the healthy functioning of the brain. Together, the brain, the mental realm/mind, and the higher self gives us access to Intuitive Power.

For the purpose of this book, to awaken woman's embodied power, mental power is not one of the topics I explore in depth because women have had enormous practice in this realm, practically to the exclusion of the fountains of feminine wisdom we do discuss here: sensual, emotional, and intuitive. However, we can use our mental abilities to enhance all the other dimensions of our being. The ability to witness is in itself a faculty of the mind. Were it not for the thinking, consciousness, and awareness of the mind, we would not be able to identify and reflect on what's happening.

Intuitive Power includes the ability of the mind to consciously reference and decipher the wisdom of the body, the heart, and our connection to spirit. In this way, Intuitive Power engages the mind and is strongly linked to it, while bridging the gaps between body, heart, mind, and spirit.

Intuitive Power and the Sensual and Emotional Bodies

The ability of the witness to pay attention to and honor the language of the body, sensation, is essential in order to develop our Intuitive Power. The body is always speaking to us.

A woman's body is energetically vibrant, with erogenous zones throughout, unlike the male body where the erogenous energy is mainly gathered in the genitals. Looking at a map of women's erogenous zones like the one shown on page 5 you see that they spread throughout your body.

Erogenous zones are areas of high sensitivity. Stimulating those parts of a woman's body can cause and enhance arousal, sending waves of pleasurable sensation through her. Erogenous zones are like antennae, always picking up signals and transmitting them to the brain via the nervous system, which in turn triggers orgasmic reactions in the body. The brain is intimately engaged in orgasm and pleasure, and supports the functions of mental awareness that we call the mind, which as we saw above is an important faculty of intuition.

As we saw in Chapter 3, your insight awareness, the Intuitive Power's tool, can help you to access and identify emotions as information. And we saw how for some people, intuitive information actually comes in the form of emotions or feelings. With our erogenous zones spreading throughout our body sending ample cues to the brain, our emotions, mind, and body are intimately linked so there's little excuse not to resource this prolific and multifaceted wisdom.

Intuitive Craving and Personal and Transpersonal Power

Intuitive craving is our longing for more God in our lives. It's the reaching out for connection to a higher source in order to feel connected to the mystery of life and have access to the wisdom inherent in that mystery. The ability to see beyond what you can touch lends meaning and dimension to your life. Healers need to be able to access this realm to be able to see a person's wholeness when their clients cannot see it themselves. Holding this space for healing to take place is how intuition can bring healing to our own and other's lives.

Part of stepping into our power as women means awakening to how much we each matter in the grand circle of life. Though your life my seem unrelated to what's going on across the globe, not to mention across town, the reality is that regardless of how big or small a role you play in international affairs, your life, and your dance matter.

When we come to sacred circle, we share and listen to other women's stories. We're touched by the poignant, painful, and glorious lives of our sisters. Their willingness to be seen, and our own, somehow can catalyze tremendous shifts and healings and whole-ings for each other. As short a distance as across the circle, to as far as across the world, down many generations, the dance of our life impacts and informs the lives of others.

The world is a very small place now. We can communicate with someone in far off lands within seconds. So, it isn't hard to see in this way how something shared in circle can affect or change the life of someone far away—six degrees of separation, right? Perhaps, your sister, for example, witnesses your brave healing around the loss of your beloved. Her life is changed because of how she lost her partner years earlier, and there are some pieces in your healing that touch her own. She calls or emails her daughter who is living in Japan and shares her regrets at not being able to express some of what she felt when her beloved passed away. Her daughter goes to work the next day where she teaches English as a second language. One of her students just lost a dog and is very sad. When your niece speaks about her own experience of loss, the student goes home and sends her brother in Germany an email expressing her happiness that he has a dog to bond with and keep him company, and on and on and on. This is the kind of thing that happens every day. Just sitting and listening to dinner conversation, it's fascinating to hear how one topic leads to the next and the next.

But transpersonal healing occurs at an even more energetic level, where no apparent direct communication has taken place. Rupert Sheldrake called it the hundredth monkey phenomena, or morphic field theory, when there is an energetic coherence across physical barriers suggesting that information travels across lines of energy and resonant fields of consciousness. Decades later, Jean Shinoda Bolen applied this theory to women's circles and calls it the Millionth Circle claiming that once one million circles of women have gathered we will have achieved a critical mass to shift our evolutionary consciousness toward the attributes of the enlightened and divine feminine.

 Claiming your power to make a difference with your own healing is a big step in embodying leadership and feminine power.

Through a common field of energy, or web of life continuum, we are all connected, and information, healing, and transformation travels across these web strings (a term coined by eco therapist Mike Cohen) to touch the lives of plants, animals, and people that we don't even know about. When we live our life as if this were the reality, we can see how our own journey is a healing path for one another's. We are each given challenges and opportunities to learn and heal, not just for ourselves, but for each other as well. In this way, we can stop obsessing and taking everything so personally, and instead understand that we are actually just being used, by a higher power, by divine spirit, God, Goddess, the creator, whatever you prefer to call it, in order for healing to occur for the collective good.

Use me! Use ME! This is the love cry of Vividly Woman Sisters. As soon as you ask for the attention of spirit, and you ask to be used as a channel for healing, you are plugging into divine wisdom. That divine wisdom, directly routed to your intuitive awareness, is what supports your intuitive knowing. Claiming your power to make a difference with your own healing is a big step in embodying leadership and feminine power. It means that whatever occurs in your life, you're willing to offer it up as a gift of consciousness for all beings.

At one time, when I had created a refuge for myself on a remote island in Northern British Columbia, I was doing deep personal healing work and getting to know a small and creative community of people who had found themselves living this remote lifestyle on a beautiful and naturally pristine island. I was befriended by a woman named Claudia whose husband was in Japan devoted to his practice as a Zen priest. From what she confided in me, they shared little intimacy when together, and she seemed to me to be very sensually shut down. Having just broken away from a marriage where there was little sexual fulfillment on my part, I could feel Claudia's pain and numbness. To some degree it was uncomfortable to have this mirrored to me. However, creatively and spiritually she was profoundly inspiring, and I was excited about the herb garden she was designing as a labyrinth and I offered to help her out with it.

At some point, Claudia left the island to attend a training in her field of healing work and I happened to bump into her husband, Rick, who was back in town. For some reason I don't really understand, I invited him over for dinner. I actually had never met him before so it was all rather auspicious that we met in the grocery store and happened to introduce ourselves.

Rick arrived for dinner, and it didn't take long before the obvious attraction was so thick and palpable in the room, neither of us could deny it. Given that I knew the connection between Rick and Claudia was practically barren, it made it even more impossible for me to contain my own arousal, knowing that he was probably feeling pretty starved for sensual connection as well.

After spontaneously pulling the Lover's tarot card and sharing some shiatsu belly massage, the rest of the evening moved quickly to deeper intimacy.

We had a beautiful night of lovemaking before he had to leave the island again to see his son on his way back to Japan. It was all a whirlwind of emotions and sexual excitement that defied my intellectual understanding. When Claudia returned, I was away, but when I got back to the island, she had already learned of the sexual encounter that had occurred between her husband and me. Rick had shared it himself and together they decided it was indeed time to separate.

Hesitant about what Claudia would think of me and that she would blame me for the break up of their marriage, I accepted her invitation to meet at her house. Claudia and I spoke about what had occurred and the tremendous relief and gratitude she felt for me. She was certain that my role in her life was as a "sacred prostitute," sent by spirit to help her heal and release from a long and painful marriage.

Accepting my role as a sacred prostitute brought me into the experience of being used by spirit for something much greater than myself, and even greater than Claudia and Rick. I was used by spirit at a transpersonal level to heal all women of the heartache of unfulfilling emotional and sexual partnership, and the generations of pain that have accumulated that anguish.

One of the trademarks of the Vividly Woman Embodied Leader Training is that we claim the power of being used by source through our dance for the healing of all women. Not only do we practice sacred dance rituals for this purpose at our live events, we also dive into being used by spirit through a fundraising and awareness raising program I conceived and birthed called the Daily Dance For Darfur and one for Rwanda as well. The Daily Dance aids women in each of those countries who've been the victims of sexual violence as a weapon of war, women who have lost everything; their family, their homes, their dignity. After soliciting sponsorships, participants dance fifteen minutes each day for a month. At first it's easy and fun to dance each day. At about day three or four we start to have to remind ourselves to dance, and we do it because we said we would, and it's for a good cause. At around day eight or nine, you're lying in bed, just about to doze off, and then you suddenly remember that you didn't dance today. "I'll dance twice as long tomorrow" you bargain with yourself. And then you get it. You get, how sweet is your life that your biggest problem is having to get out of bed and dance for fifteen minutes for women who have suffered profound loss and violence and don't have that same privilege. So you get up, and you dance, and you get, in every fibre of your beautiful body temple, how much your dance really can matter. Perhaps one of the most powerful statements we can make is: *My body is a vessel for healing and I offer my dance for my sisters who cannot dance for themselves.* When you know this with your own flesh and bones, you have touched a dimension of leadership that will stir you and others to their core.

Intuitive Power and Choice

When we venture into the realm of Intuitive Power, many aspects of intuition come to mind. Does this mean psychic power, does this refer to being able to predict the future or communicate with entities? These are the associations that often arise when we use the term intuition in our culture because often intuition is employed when there is a difficult decision to be made.

When our intuition speaks to us, we have a decision to make: whether to listen to it or not. Likewise, when we have a decision to make, our intuition speaks, providing us with a choice option. Intuition and decision making go hand in hand.

Intuitive knowing is distinct from ego knowing. Intuitive Power is the discipline to be guided by intuitive knowing. The ability to distinguish ego from intuition is an essential skill that provides us enormous blessings and life fulfillment, the experience of being spiritually aligned and in our highest integrity.

Intuitive Power is related to our connection to a deep reverent source of wisdom that resides within us or is sourced from our higher self, versus preferences and ideals imposed on us from the outside world, family, society, our peers. Intuitive wisdom is our truth that is either conscious or unconscious. When we begin listening to the inner voices of truth, we are not only hearing those truths, we are also listening to them and for them.

Hearing truth and developing the habit of listening inwardly for it has been profoundly encouraged for me by the time I spend in nature. Multi-day wilderness outings with some of my best girlfriends each year for the last fifteen have been wonderful times for nourishing my awareness of the inner voice of truth. Every trip is a new adventure in our relationship to nature, to our bodies, and to each other. We are witnessing the evolution of our lives and the passage of time from one trip to the next. On one such trip, we were kayaking in Nootkah Sound, off the west coast of Vancouver Island.

It was late June, and summer had not yet made its appearance. Weather, gear, and creature comfort/safety issues were not synchronizing, which caused the trip to be particularly challenging. The need to get along, not rock the boat, and not miss the opportunity to get the most out of the adventure were all at play on the trip, which took us to almost the northernmost tip of the Island.

It was windy, rainy, and cold. I wasn't feeling great about leaving the safe haven of our camping spot. I would have preferred to not venture out. But one of my dear sisters, Kara, always the risk-taker, was avidly trying to convince us that we should get out there and do what we went there to do—kayak.

I didn't want to be a stick in the mud, but my intuition told me to stay put and not risk the weather, given my flimsy gear. But was it really intuition, or was it fear? And is there even a difference?

Ultimately, the decision was made to play it safe, so with the time to linger, we launched into a verbal exploration of intuition and fear.

The above is a typical scenario, that may seem out of the ordinary because we are dealing with a potentially life or health threatening situation, but the truth is that we are always making decisions all day long informed by our intuitive voices and impulses, and our fears.

Fear is a voice unto itself. Some people use fear as an indication of what to move toward instead of away from. Those individuals who are especially addicted to adrenal rush will gravitate toward what gives them the rush and gets them feeling alive. Is this an intuitive hit?

For those like me, who run from feelings of fear and use fear as an indicator of what to avoid, fear can be one of the myriad voices that informs my intuition. There are instinctual fears, and there are learned fears, and they can be interwoven and interchangeable. Perhaps what's most important is not only to be able to distinguish between fear and intuition, but to be able to appreciate them both and discover their interface and the way they influence one another.

Intuition is often interpreted as a pristine faculty that has a clear intent and practical intention. I either am or am not listening to my intuition, and if things go awry, I clearly have not heeded my intuition. But what if, instead of there being a right or wrong choice to be made, intuition guides us along the way and is only measured by our level of personal integrity. What if outer circumstances are not the measurement of Intuitive Power? What if personal integrity is the real thermostat of our level of intimate connection to our intuition? What if the truth of how I feel, what I sense, and the experience of being at peace are the truest and only real way to measure intuition?

Picking up on my kayaking story is an example. I didn't feel at ease kayaking the channel during the poor weather. The wind was picking up. It felt like it was beyond my skill level to take that on. I felt fear at the thought of crossing, and I sensed it in my throat. If I absolutely had to do it or was already in the center of the channel and the wind whipped up, I could probably have made it. But it would have been a lot of work, would have created more fear and stress, and would have been very uncomfortable, turning a fun girls' adventure into a nightmare of an experience. I didn't feel peace within me about creating the possibility of those circumstances for myself. Intuitively, I knew that was not how I would feel most at ease with myself, and feeling ill at ease with myself or out of integrity with what I most wanted and needed for peace of mind was the antithesis of what I went on the trip for.

What gets in the way?

Being fully in my Intuitive Power means resourcing the wisdom of my Crone, the witnessing awareness that sees and perceives all of what I cannot see and touch on the physical plane.

Why can't I see this more tangibly? Why can't I know for sure the way I can be sure what color the sky is or what sound an eagle makes? Why do I question my Intuitive Power, and then suffer for not being in tune with my truth.

> *Intuitive Power Exercise*
>
> Here are some questions to ask yourself for personal inquiry into why your Intuitive Power feels limited or hindered.
>
> Who told me not to trust my intuition?
>
> Who made the decisions in my childhood?
>
> What would happen if I followed my intuition for a full day, week or month?

> Whose love would I have risked if I followed my intuition?
>
> Who are the role models of those who follow their intuition?
>
> When was the last time I listened to my intuitive knowing?
>
> When was the last time I didn't listen?
>
> Have I forgiven myself for not listening?
>
> Can I learn to forgive myself when I don't listen and appreciate when I do without making myself right or wrong?

Intuition and Ego

Ego wants something. It is completely subjectively engaged and has us believe there is a right and wrong choice, which is why decision-making can be difficult; we fear making the "wrong" decision. Ego has an investment both in making the "right" choice and in the outcome, not for the outcome itself, but for what the outcome will mean or catalyze. My interaction with my promoter, Fiona, is a good example of this. My ego was invested in getting recognition, not for the sake of recognition, but because it would prove my self-worth.

Intuition, on the other hand, is completely objective. There is no inherently right or wrong outcome; there is only the outcome. What matters most is being in integrity with one's self versus satisfying the need of the ego being right. Personal integrity has a distinctive peace of mind quality about it that is not an inherent aspect of ego. When we seek out peace of mind, personal integrity is naturally nourished. The more personal integrity is nourished, the more Intuitive Power is encouraged. A circle Sister once shared that years earlier her car broke down on a deserted country road while driving with her young child. She quickly locked the doors when a Hell's Angel turned up and approached the car. Her intuition told her to protect herself and her child from this burly stranger. The fact that he ended up changing her tire and guiding her to the nearest garage does not imply that her intuition was wrong, it simply means that without being able to fortune tell the future, a mother's intuition would naturally have her taking precautions to keep her and her child safe.

Try this exercise to identify your felt Sense experience of ego vs. intuition. Once you get the hang of it you'll have an easy to access tool that will support you to resource intuition and be able to recognize it when it's speaking to you.

Ego vs. Intuition Practice

1. Identify a decision that you need to make. It should be something you've been struggling with deciding. If you weren't struggling with it you would already have made the decision. Most likely your intuition and your ego are at odds.
2. Identify your choice options and write them down.
3. Beside each option write what your attraction is to that option. Notice which option is ego driven and which is intuition driven.
4. One at a time bring each option in to your awareness and ask yourself where it lives in your body and the quality of the sensation. We call this the practice of *Body Sourcing* and we'll explore it more in Chapter 11—Somatic Lens.

> This practice will give you a taste of the felt Sense experience of ego in your body and the felt Sense experience of intuition in your body so you can recognize each more easily.

The Light and Shadow of Intuitive Power

When you're enrolling the light aspect of your Intuitive Power, you refer to your intuition for insight and information that you include with the facts and knowledge that are available to you. You use your intuitive awareness to leverage the hard tangible truth, instead of the other way around.

It was fall in northern California where, Jill, her husband, and young son lived. Events of late had placed stress on their marriage and both Jill and her husband were in a doubting place about their future together. Was their three-year marriage worth hanging in there for? Who hasn't wondered this a time or two during the course of a relationship?

Jill had a reading with a psychic who told her that she would be enjoying a new primary relationship in the spring. Instead of taking that to mean that she and her husband would split up, which didn't intuitively fit for her, she listened to her own inner voice and interpreted the psychic's premonition to mean that she and her husband would be moving to new heights and establishing a new and improved dimension of their marriage. Come that spring, and now two years later, Jill and her husband are still together devoted to the life of their marriage.

The shadow side of Intuitive Power expresses itself when you defer to your intuition, God, or other intuitive authorities and blame them when things go awry. The shadow also expresses itself when you evangelize in the name of spiritual wisdom and impose your beliefs on others.

Intuitive Power at Work

Intuitive power is an integral part of our daily work lives in as much as just about every action we take is preceded by a decision whether to act or not, or which action to take among the myriad options available to us. Making decisions, as we've seen above, so often takes us into the dance of distinguishing what is the best decision to make, or more accurately what is the "right" decision. Having a clear sense of what is driving you, ego or intuition, will be a valuable tool to take the mystery and the misery out of this daily dance.

Decisions begin with the first seconds of awakening each morning, and continue until we at last drift off to sleep at night. Making business decisions with greater ease and clarity relieves us of tremendous struggle and strife. Not a day or an hour goes by that you don't have to choose between listening to your ego or following your intuition. Having a vivid felt sense awareness of each is a powerful compass to guide your way.

Intuitive Power and the Textures

Intuitive Power relates primarily to the fifth Vividly Woman texture, Express. Here we discover that to express ourselves authentically in our pristine integrity is to be a channel for higher self-wisdom that connects us to source and universal life intelligence.

Intuitive Power Activism

Ultimately, to be so passionate that you can't not strive for growth and change at the social, political, economical or environmental level always requires a strong calling of one's higher self. All activists embody intuitive power because they are being used and are working for something bigger than themselves. There is one woman who in particular stands out for me because she's had a significant voice in the revival of earth-based spiritual activism and Goddess religion which she's helped to creatively weave into the world of political activism. Starhawk, author, song writer, founder of Earth Activists Training, channels her passion for ecological systems thinking prolifically through her writing and innovative teaching techniques across the globe.

Chapter 4 Summary: Intuitive Power

~ Intuition is awareness and acknowledgement of higher self-truth. It's what we know but often ignore because it may be in contrast to what the ego wants.

~ Repeated blind sighting sends a message to your intuition that you don't trust it, and thus its voice becomes less and less audible.

~ Intuition and decision making go hand in hand.

~ When we begin paying attention to the inner voices of truth, we are not only hearing those truths, we are also listening to them and listening for them.

~ When we seek out and are motivated by peace of mind, personal integrity is nourished. The more personal integrity is nourished, the more Intuitive Power is encouraged.

~ Part of stepping into our power as women means awakening to how much we each matter in the larger scheme of things, claiming not only our personal but our transpersonal power as well.

~ The light aspect of intuition is when you use your intuitive awareness to leverage the hard tangible truth, instead of the other way around.

~ The Intuitive Power Goddess archetype is the Crone and her ability to see objectively and be informed by her rich life experience.

**To arouse your embodied power,
visit our "Intuitive Power" stimulators at**

www.VividlyWoman.com

TEXTURES

Mature Energy Management

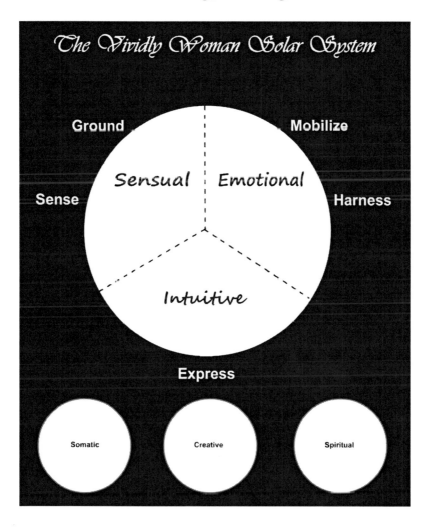

> *"Within my body are all the sacred places of the world, and the most profound pilgrimage I can ever make is within my own body."*
> —Saraha

CHAPTER 5

Sense

Awareness is the Foundation of Your Journey

With a basic understanding of the first dimension and heart of the Vividly Woman Solar System: the power centers, Sensual, Emotional and Intuitive, we're ready to explore the second dimension: the textures or *planets* that constellate around the sun or solar center. This collection of five textures: Sense, Ground, Mobilize, Harness, and Express is a system unto itself that we use as a road map to explore and discover ourselves as energetic beings flowing through a natural energy continuum. Energy has an inherent behavioral pattern, a path of least resistance that offers us freedom, flow, and fruition. When we tap into and leverage this innate wellspring we are in synch with the order of the universe and can enjoy its gifts.

The textures, like planets, each have a relationship to the central core of the system and predominantly relate to and lead us into more intimate embodiment of the power center closest to the texture on the solar system schematic. The five textures each have unique and distinctive qualities and mysteries. We'll look at each on their own and also how they dance with each other.

Sense, the first texture, is aptly so, because it's only through our sensing awareness and presence that we can hope to have an experiential, rather than merely a conceptual understanding of the textures. Here in Sense, we begin to unveil layers of subtle awakening that enrich our existence beyond just being an observer, to being a subjective companion of all experiences.

Women, whether we intend it or not, have a profound connection to the world of sensory stimulation. We are enchanted and engaged by our senses in many unconscious as well as conscious ways. Perhaps it's because of the elaborate erogenous aliveness of our body, compared to the more concentrated erogenous area of a man's body, that gives women this wealth of sensual abundance.

Our senses give us access to a rich world of stimulation that's beyond what our rational minds conjure up. Thankfully, some things, like the senses are beyond human invention. And while we can augment sensory stimulation from the outside through external influences, we can also enhance and amplify sensation from the inside through inner attention.

In addition to acute awareness of sensation, we also have the ability to blend our senses. Synesthesia is a quality of experience in which the senses merge, taking on each other's characteristics and expanding in their effect. Marijuana, an external source, has a strong ability to encourage synesthesia through its ability to slow the perception of time. In this state, we are more present for the minute details that typically escape our conscious awareness. Synesthesia allows us to smell colors, to enjoy the textures of sounds, and listen to tastes. Synesthesia is not wild imagination; it is a way to access a part of the brain that has greater sensory possibilities.

The Vividly Woman texture, Sense, encourages us to venture into that depth of experiencing the senses without the use of drugs, so that our communion with our everyday life is facilitated, amplified, and enriched.

Communion

Our senses are a profound opportunity to enter into sacred communion with the world around us.

Shawna, a member of the Vividly Woman online community explored Sense through the monthly curriculum and this was part of what she shared,

"A very powerful part of the Vividly Woman curriculum for me has been making sensory connections in nature. I have always felt drawn to natural things and been at home in nature, but I haven't really analysed this before. Now, the time I spend in nature is turning up the volume of my senses. I want to savour the experience and commune with nature rather than rushing through a twenty-minute jog or chatting with other dog walkers."

The extent of our ability to enter into communion with rather than observe through our sensing awareness, is further expressed through Shawna's words.

"So when it came to sensually choosing an ally in nature for the exercise in the Vividly Woman curriculum last month, it was no surprise to me that my ally was a tree in this forest. I had admired this particular tree before—a tall slender tree with four branching trunks, swathed in a sensual green velvet gown of moss. This tree radiates calm energy, compassion, empathy, and strength. In the exercise, I wrote of this tree and my connection with it:

"Your roots are your senses, connecting you to the earth mother and the surrounding forest—drawing nutrients to your heart, which spills open with love and compassion. Your branches lift to the sky in gratitude and expectation—open and bare, but for a few jewel-like leaves clinging in beauteous space, like coloured beads. All clutter has dropped away—only the jewels remain for all to see. Look at the life you support! The ferns and moss clinging to your trunks and branches give you texture and add to your beauty . . . harmonious symbiosis."

The level of intimacy of our communion with nature and all of life experience is dictated by not just the level of sensory perception you have about the quality of the world around you, but is more dependent on the quality of perception you have of the corresponding universe of sensation inside of you. This is your truth in each moment and paying attention to this information is what we call being *self-referring*. The extent to which you refer inwardly for your answers versus referring to the outside world, will determine your level of authenticity and integrity with yourself.

 Direct your sensing awareness inwardly as well as outwardly.

I remember the very first time I attended a class in body/mind awareness. It was back in the late 1980's when I still lived in Montreal. I was waitressing in a hip teahouse restaurant and met a French gentleman named Philippe Leblanc who invited me to attend a class he was teaching called Feldenkrais. I didn't know anything about it, but I knew it was different from the world I was surrounded by and that I was due to shake that up a bit.

The class was harmless enough. We learned that if we moved our body mechanically without purpose, we had limited range of motion. If we moved using our imagination in service of our purpose, the simplest movement required less strain, and we had more maneuverability in a healthier way.

I signed up for the eight-week series, and I enjoyed the introduction to something radically different than I'd ever encountered. Around week three, Philippe led us through the exercises as he did each week, allowing us to follow along by merely listening to his instructions rather than watching him. In this way, we could each honor our own unique interpretation of his directions. On this particular evening, we were lying on our backs on a mat. After a series of movements, he instructed us to open our mouths and stick out our tongues. "Open your mouth as wide as possible, and stick your tongue out as far as possible," he said. I instantly became suspicious. Why did he want me to stick out my tongue? What kind of a pervert was this man? I opened my mouth slightly wider, but even at that, only the tip of my tongue emerged from behind my lips. I was paralyzed and opened my eyes to look around to try and see what the others in the class were doing. They were doing it! Try as I might, though, I could not let myself open my mouth to its fullest capacity and expose my tongue completely. I just couldn't.

Today, I look back on that experience and laugh. Now, it seems ridiculous to me that I was paranoid about this being some kind of sexual ploy. But at the time, it was a profound illustration of just how hyper dependent I was on how I might look to the world around me to the exclusion of being able to actually sense into what the experience elicited at a sensual vs. a mental level. Little did I know this issue, being externally or internally referring, would become something that would preoccupy me enormously in the years to come.

Though we didn't all have this exact experience, most of the women I meet in Vividly Woman circles, on some level have shut down their sensuality in order to protect themselves from what others might think, say, and do. The texture of Sense invites us to reclaim sensing awareness and sensory relating on our own terms instead of within the limits of what is acceptable by others.

When you're deeply engaged at a sensory level, having a sensing relationship with the world around you and inside of you, you're experiencing a profound level of authentic presence that enriches your life. When you experience life at a cursory level, skimming over your surroundings and stimulus, your life begins to pale and lacks luster. The analogy I like is one of riding in an air conditioned tour bus with tinted windows and watching the tropical rain forest go by, as opposed to being out in the humid, vividly erupting sound and color of it all with my own body. These are two radically different encounters that will determine the quality of one's life.

Let's look at how the senses can take us inward instead of being a distraction.

I Feel, I Sense

I arrive at a dance class all ready to move till I'm soaked. Instead, the teacher is facilitating a gentle and slow moving floor play class. I'm disappointed and irritated. I consider leaving I'm so annoyed. I came wanting to dance, not roll around on the ground like an amoeba. Instead of instantly taking off, I decide to check in with what's happening inside me. I know that this experience is a pretty innocuous one in the scheme of things, so when I notice the tension, anxiety and blame stewing inside of me and its felt Sense texture of inner tightness in my throat and chest, it's clear to me that what I'm feeling and sensing have nothing to do with the situation at hand and that blaming the teacher is clearly not going to reduce my discomfort.

 I can choose to honor the sensations that correspond to my feelings by acknowledging what I sense, without needing a reason to justify them.

I could come up with any other number of reasons why I'm feeling this way that I've displaced or suppressed. Instead, through my learned practice of *I Feel, I Sense* I just allow the sensations to be what they are and attend to them by staying in my body, instead of trying to figure out why I'm having them, which would take me out of my body into my head. I honor the emotions by acknowledging what I feel and I honor the sensations that correspond to the feelings by acknowledging what I sense, without needing a reason for them. In essence, I'm focusing on my body sensations instead of the story that would justify them. It sounds something like this: I feel frustrated and I sense that in my chest.

I understand that a good part of this experience is from some other part of my life, an unresolved issue from some time somewhere that's rising to the surface now. Will identifying that issue guarantee that I will stop suffering? No, in the past it has not, and it has actually made my suffering worse. So I stay with the sensation. I allow it to breathe itself through me, and give it space to expand and ultimately dissolve. The practice of *I Feel, I Sense,* a Vividly Woman "staple" allows me to honor my experience without indulging it and dragging it out unnecessarily. This practice has relieved me of suffering many times over the years. Instead of stewing over issues, I attend to them through my body and am able to move on quickly instead of obsessing and agonizing endlessly.

Just as each emotion registers as a sensation in your body, each sensing relationship that we have in our encounters with the world outside us has a corresponding sensory experience occurring within us. For instance, as I look at the sky I'm having a relationship with it through my sense of sight and my body is registering that encounter as a felt Sense experience of spaciousness and calm. We are constantly making choices and decisions about our relationship to the world, largely at an unconscious level, oblivious of what our body sensations are telling us. Our inner response to the color green is different than our inner response to the color orange. The kaleidoscope of stimulation that we are constantly being bombarded with in the big and busy world we live in is having enormous effect on us at a sensation level. If we listen inwardly and attend to our inner responses we are in a current relationship and more present with our inner truth.

Eccentric eco therapy Guru Michael Cohen, says there are many more than just five senses. He's identified fifty-three. Along with sight, sound, smell, touch, and taste, Michael shows us that gravity is a sense, temperature is a sense, and light and dark are senses, as are space and color. All these sensing awarenesses are stimulating sensation within us.

For years I lived in a quiet community on a peninsula in British Columbia. There was little traffic, only one traffic light on a forty-five mile long coastline. The world danced much more slowly and patiently there. After several years living in this way, I became entrained with its rhythm. To entrain means to actually resonate energetically with an outside body at the same frequency.

This was not normally apparent to me because I was absorbed in the experience, oblivious of anything else. However, when I would go into the big city, about an hour's trip south by ferry and car, I noticed myself feeling ill at ease and out of synch with the external world there. I did what I needed to do and got myself back home as quickly as possible.

After ten years living in this remote place, my life choices brought me back to living in the city. At first, I was keenly aware of how my inner rhythm was very different from that of the rhythm around me. I actually sensed myself as an outside observer to the busy hum of life rather than an engaged participant. I was not yet entrained. Slowly over the course of about six months, I became completely immersed and I was fully in synch with that vibration and could no longer perceive it because I *was* it. We'll explore this further as we look at the Vividly Woman practice of *Sensual Resonance* next.

Sensual Resonance

Sense is a valuable tool when we're endeavoring to manifest and achieve specific results. We use it in this goal oriented way in the VividExistence Coaching System, a linear adjunct to the Vividly Woman work.

The use of Sense in this context is based on the understanding that to merely want or need something to materialize for us is pale in comparison to resonating with that goal or result on a sensual level. If you can attain a similar vibration to that which you are calling in, you'll be way more likely to attract it to you. For that reason, we use each of the five senses to identify where in our body we are already resonating with the goal, and what the shared quality is that we are already embodying. Claiming that connection as already existing sends an energetic message to the universe that you are a friendly container for what you're asking for. The next time you find yourself pining for a thing or striving to reach a goal, try this exercise:

Sensual Resonance Practice

My Goal: _____

Taste
My goal tastes like _____
This taste lives in my _____
The quality of its sensation is _____

Texture
My texture of my goal is _____
This texture lives in my _____
The quality of its sensation is _____

Smell
My goal smells like _____
This fragrance lives in my _____
The quality of its sensation is _____

Sight
My goal looks like _____
This visual lives in my _____
The quality of its sensation is _____

Sound
My goal sounds like _____
This sound lives in my _____
The quality of its sensation is _____

Body Sourcing

"*Body Sourcing* is my favorite method of decision-making . . . the only one that works every time," Helena, Vividly Woman Coach Trainee

At the heart of the Vividly Woman work is our practice of *Body Sourcing*—turning inward to identify felt Sense experience instead of engaging in the stories of the mind. Though we explore emotions and spirit, we constantly ask the body for its take on what's happening so that we can be in touch with the pristine truth instead of manipulated interpretations.

One of our coach trainees, Glenys, shared her homework experience of practicing body sourcing. Here's what she had to say about working with her client's healing process: "At one point I asked her to pause because her story began to be more important than the emotions that she was feeling. I asked her to take a few breaths and notice where she was sensing the emotions in her body, and I acknowledged her emotions by thanking her for sharing."

Your body and your ability to sense its textural utterances have the potential to provide you with valuable insight and wise reflections that can help you avoid mental and emotional pain and anguish as much as possible. Most often, you're given the message that what your body is experiencing is not so terrifying after all. Therefore, you needn't run from it up into your head's analysis. Instead, what's required is gentle tenderness and self-care to soothe and dissolve what's troubling you. It doesn't mean the issue will vanish, but at least any debilitating judgments and self-inflicted blame you have won't consume you and exacerbate the situation.

As we'll see in Chapter 11—Somatic Lens, we use these two questions to access the information of the body:

Questions

Where do I sense it in my body?

What is the quality of the sensation?

Sense, the Somatic Lens, and Sensual Power, though belonging to different dimensions of the Vividly Woman Solar System, are closely connected and intertwined. We might say that they are unique branches sourced from the same root. Each of them inspires us to connect to our inner sensing awareness. This is an important foundation to have established as we enter into a discussion about boundaries.

Boundaries

It's no secret that women can find it challenging to maintain a distinct and authentic sense of self in relationships, both personal and professional. Finding yourself betraying your own true needs and preferences to accommodate another's in order to keep the peace, avoid abandonment, or just because we've been taught that it's a woman's job to sacrifice for the relationship, is so common in our world it's something we almost take for granted.

When I bring up the topic of boundaries at the live Vividly Woman workshops and retreats that make up the Embodied Leader Training, it's almost like I'm speaking a foreign language. "A boundary, what's that?" or "I thought intimacy was about letting others in, not keeping them out."

The misunderstandings and lack of familiarity about boundaries is precisely why I bring them up at the beginning of each training. Establishing felt Sense boundary awareness is what facilitates a sense of self that is the basis for inner work. In other words, without a sense of boundaries, there isn't really a self to explore and do inquiry about.

You might be wondering, so what is a boundary if it's not a wall to keep others out?

A boundary is the periphery of the energetic field that emanates from your center 360 degrees around your body and orients you in the world in relationship to other beings, things, and situations. Imagine yourself standing in the center of a hula-hoop. The hoop can be any circumference. The hoop is a physical representation of your energy boundary.

When our boundaries are intact we feel a sense of well-being, autonomy, and a quality of "I am-ness," When our boundaries have been crashed into by another, or if we fail to consciously set our own boundaries, we can become disconnected from our center, unsettled in our own skin, stuck in our energy, less potent and powerful.

Healthy boundaries are alive and ever changing. They change to accommodate circumstances, moods, and current needs. Knowing this is essential. Expect your boundaries to organically shift if they are an authentic expression of you. This is your body and your energy speaking to you. A healthy boundary can and does change. The ability to alter our own energetic field in response to our interactions based on what our body perceives about current conditions, is an expression of our boundary awareness.

When I'm speaking or presenting to a large group, I establish a larger boundary than when I'm being sexually intimate with my husband, when my boundary is much smaller because the connection is more intimate. Stepping on to a stage with hundreds of people in the audience demands that I bring with me a boundary that commands attention, and takes up space.

Rather than being a wall to keep people or things out, a boundary is like a container that allows you to have more of you. While boundaries can be misconstrued as separating us from each other, the truth is that when we learn how to have healthy and distinctive boundaries, we can be more truly present with each other, and more authentically connected. It's important to understand the meaning of having authentic boundaries because then we'll be more naturally motivated to create them.

I learned a lot about boundaries in my years living in British Columbia when I had the blessing of regular therapy with an Integrative Body Psychotherapist, and my subsequent years of study in that same modality. Working one on one with my therapist, Mary, each of us stayed authentic to our true boundary by creating a circle around ourselves with string. We had the freedom to change the size of the boundary when and if we sensed the need to. I developed the habit of staying aware of my boundaries through the container that we created of honesty and reverence for our needs in each moment.

Though I don't often have the occasion to create a physical boundary around myself using yarn or string, an energetic version works just as well once you get the hang of it. When I work with groups and individuals in Mexico, we sit on the sand and draw a circle in the sand, which works great too.

 Consciously creating my boundary brings me home to my power.

When I teach, present or facilitate group process, I notice that the way I relate to and the way that the group perceives me, is strongly influenced by my ability to stay conscious of my boundary. Without a sense of my own boundary I'll often feel unsure of being able to hold the space for the group, most likely because I am not even really holding the space for myself. When first I hold the space for me, by consciously creating my own boundary, there's an instant sense of *coming home* in my body. This connection to myself is what it means to be in my power. From this place I can hold a reverent and dynamic space for others, inspiring them to trust in my leadership.

Types of Boundaries

Boundaries can be fluid, fixed, contracted, and expanded. Most likely we all experience a little of each at different moments, in different situations, with different individuals, etc. Just as the dance of life ebbs and flows, boundaries ebb and flow as well.

A fluid boundary flows and changes according to the situation. A fixed boundary is rigid and does not easily accommodate changing circumstances. A contracted boundary causes one to shrink back, shut down, and/or lose power. An expanded boundary may cause one to be overbearing, approval seeking, and/or lose a realistic sense of oneself.

By now you should be getting a sense of how true boundaries are always an authentic expression of you. The meaning of honoring authentic boundaries in your life is valuable beyond measure because it will show up in every relationship and impact all outcomes.

Fear of letting someone down is fear of having clear boundaries because you're afraid you might lose love. In the end though, you end up feeling resentful, which causes distance in your relationship, the opposite of what you want.

I saw this dynamic happen within the Vividly Woman organization. One of the Vividly Woman Embodied Leader graduates, Jenna, stepped into the role of co-facilitator early on in the co-facilitator program. She was one of the first to venture forward in this capacity, and in so doing, she helped to blaze the trail for others to come and I'll always appreciate her immensely for her devotion and courage.

However, Jenna, in her desire to be an amazing co-facilitator, which she was, and as many women do, bit off way more than she could chew, leaving her private counseling practice suffering. After a year showing up, exceeding everyone's expectations, she finally drew a line and created a boundary that for me felt like a reaction to not having had a boundary soon enough, causing a boomerang-like need to step down from her role. I was so sorry to lose her, yet fully supported her need to be true to herself.

Boundaries are not something that others are responsible for creating for you. Only you can create the energetic space that authentically fits your needs. In the words of Vividly Woman Embodied Leader Graduate, Catriona, "I used to think that the lack of respecting my boundaries by another person was something done to me; now I understand that I create my own boundaries which set the parameters for how others treat me (they are an inside-out experience)."

We'll explore more about boundaries in relationships in Chapter 8—Harness.

Sense Goddess

The West African Goddess Oshun embodies the essence of Sense. Oshun governs rivers, beauty, and sensuality and is said to signal the awakening of sensuality through beauty and art, sensual delights, and self-adornment. Oshun calls upon mirrors, aromatherapy, scented baths, jewelry, honey, golden silks, feathers, and colorful scarves to awaken the senses.

The meandering of the river symbolizes her sensuously female movements.

Sense Icon

Marilyn Monroe's Hollywood persona is an extreme example of Sense. Portrayed as oozing with sexual, sensual Eros, Marilyn was a culture's projection of what feminine sensuality could and should look like in the 1950's and early 1960's.

Other Sense icons contributed by Vividly Woman Sisters are Cleopatra, Beyonce', and Georgia O'Keeffe.

Sense at Work

As we saw in the practice of Sensual Resonance, sensing what we intend to manifest is a powerful way to attract our desires to us. Sense at work is very much in alignment with that. You see, the sense stage of anything is the visioning, imagining or conception phase of an endeavor. It's the place where we dare to dream what we're being called to birth. But far beyond merely coming up with a great idea and letting it simmer, we take an active role in its gestation by sensually aligning with it.

Using your 5 senses and embodying the outcome you desire, Sense packs a powerful punch to get you on the road to realizing what was once only a dream. Whether you are in the gestation phase or are already up and running and headed for your next level of achievement, Sense will bring you into energetic synchronicity with your aspirations for your product or service. Sense makes sure that you're vibrating at the same frequency of a successful venture so that you attract more success to you.

Sense in Relationship to the Other Textures

The key word for Sense in relationship to the other textures is *awareness*. Sense gives us a felt awareness versus conceptual understanding of each of the other textures when we're dancing with them. Remember to resource your sensing awareness as we journey onward through the remaining four textures for a depth experience of each. Awareness of the home within is a big first step in finding our way back there. A woman's way home is made easier to navigate with the awareness that Sense inspires.

Chapter 5 Summary: Sense

~ The texture of Sense helps us to unveil layers of subtle awakening that enrich our existence beyond just being observer, to being a subjective companion of all experiences.

~ The quality of perception you have of the universe of sensation inside of you, your truth in each moment, and paying attention to this information is what constitutes being self-referring.

~ The texture of Sense invites us to reclaim sensing awareness and sensory relating on our own terms instead of within the limits of what is acceptable by others.

~ For every emotion you feel and sensing relationship you have there's a corresponding sensation in your body.

~ Expect your boundaries to organically shift if they are an authentic expression of you.

~ Rather than being a wall to keep people or things out, a boundary is like a container that allows you to have more space for more of *you* and for more intimate, authentic relationships.

~ The keyword for Sense is *awareness*.

**To arouse your embodied power,
visit our "Sense" stimulators at**

www.VividlyWoman.com

> "Here on this mountain I am not alone. For all the lives I used to be are with me. All the lives tell me now I have come home."
> – Joan Halifax

CHAPTER 6

Ground

Cultivate Presence and Your Earth Body

With the awareness that we've tapped into in Sense, we can now venture into the next texture, Ground, anticipating a felt sense experience of its distinct essence.

"Sister, tell me what grounds you?" These words fill the room as each pair of sisters invites one another to answer this question.

The room in which we find ourselves is at a Vividly Woman Live Training called Embody Self Love Intensive. Nicknamed *The Excavation*, it's all about digging our true selves out from under the rubble that's been piled up, heap upon heap, obliterating our core essence so that it's become barely perceptible. We ask these questions, seemingly simple, yet piercing to the core.

In one simple question, what we are really saying is, "tell me what anchors you, body, self, and soul. Tell me what brings you home to the essence that is you, over and over again, when everything else is falling apart, spinning out of control, when chaos erupts, what truly and reliably stabilizes, orients you, and brings you home?"

These are the blessings of Ground. We Ground to give ourselves a sense of landing at home within ourselves, in relationship to the physical body that is our temple, a radiant mobile extension of the one mother that birthed us all, Mother Earth.

As such, in our relatedness and our oneness with earth, Ground takes us into the realm of gravitational connection. In order to really appreciate our connection to gravity, we must let her carry us. Surrendering into being carried by earth allows us to transfer our energy through us into her, to spread our energetic charge and have her hold it for us. This is an aspect of Ground that is contain. Connect, carry, and contain are the three C's of Ground that we'll explore in this chapter and bring living color to this wonderful texture so ripe with meaning for living in a body.

The Three C's of Grounding

Carry—let the earth carry you. Only through surrender to the earth can you harvest her gravitational field. Donna Farhi, the New Zealand born international yoga teacher, trainer, and author of several yoga books, teaches us that there is a subtle balance between collapsing, becoming completely limp and propping, or resisting earth's energetic pull. This subtle in-between place is where we can still resource earth energy but not be consumed by it. She calls this place yielding.

Contain—Honor your body as a sacred temple that contains your spirit, inspiring a safe vessel that you inhabit where you can practice awareness, love and tender care. In circle, we foster a sacredness that is a precious container where we feel safe to speak our truth and practice loving presence, allowing each sister to have her truth without our judgment of it. In our life we create a safe container by living in the moment, and acknowledging our feelings and sensations.

Later in Chapter 8—Harness, you'll see how this will be an essential part of how you harness energy in order to grow and expand it.

Connect—As you connect to the earth, you connect to your body, and vice versa. Grounding necessitates relationship and communication in order for the reciprocity inherent in connect to occur. Being connected to earth is one aspect of connect in Ground. Another aspect is being connected to our own self. Being present in our body, when the mind and body are aligned, is another way of saying that we are grounded in our body versus being fragmented or split off.

Much of the work that I did in therapy was centered on learning to identify when I was connected to or present in, my body, and when I was no longer there because my mind had left my body. Leaving my body was a chronic habit of mine and it was fascinating to witness the frequency with which I abandoned my body and went somewhere else. Mary, my therapist supported me through many life dramas over the years of our working together, but as far as I'm concerned they were all just devices for me to get more conscious of my tendency to *split off* and to be able to track that behavior so I could be in conscious choice about it.

Home

In Ground we give form to the energy of Sense. Like formulating a tangible plan from an idea, or mapping out a series of steps to manifestation on the physical plain, the felt Sense experience of Ground is revealed to us when we consciously resource earth's gravitational power and when we acknowledge ourselves as spirit being expressed in physical form.

 Grounding in the home within you and tending to life's daily tasks don't have to be mutually exclusive.

Finding the home within is a profound way to get acquainted with the texture of Ground. The Home within stays constant and grounded when all else is subject to change. Life can destabilize us and make us forget our sense of home. Working hard to achieve success, raising a family, making ends meet, living up to standards and approval from outside yourself can all take their toll on the connection of home to the woman within you. Although grounding in the home within you and tending to life's daily tasks don't have to be mutually exclusive you may often find yourself behaving as if they are. Coming home for women devoted to living our creative embodied power is about having both a strong sense of honoring our authentic truth AND fulfilling all our responsibilities as a householder.

This excerpt from my journal captures a facet of my own experience of discovering the true constant of home within me:

> After over a year of living like a gypsy, without a home base, I have truly birthed into the comfort of knowing the home within. For several months I had judgments and discomfort with this situation of being without a physical home. I struggled and bemoaned what I missed in the way of familiarity and convenience. What I would only give for my own walk-in closet! Now, knowing instinctively that a physical home will be mine again someday, I surrender into my current reality, which is to live like a Bedouin, or a turtle,

taking my home with me from place to place. Locating the sensations of home within me helps to orient myself in the loving embrace of all of creation, knowing that I am always being cared for at the very deepest level.

Finding the home within is not a finite exercise. It's a practice of over and over turning inward and making your inner truth *the* truth! As you cultivate an awareness of and intimacy with yourself as a spiritual being living in a physical body, you discover that you are never alone. In the words of Abraham, channeled by Jerry and Esther Hicks, "At the root of your physical condition is the condition of your cells. At the root of the physical condition of your cells is a Vibrational pattern. At the root of that Vibrational pattern is alignment with the Well-Being of the Source within you."

Your body is a temple, and within it lives the spirit self that connects you to all of life, the infinite wisdom, the absolute truth and authenticity that the home within you embodies. Orienting yourself in the essence of this home is the ultimate gift of Ground. However, in order to claim this gift, you need to know what Ground feels like in your body, and it can be helpful to know what ungrounded feels like, too.

So how do we sense Ground? It's often hard to be consciously aware of things when they are so close to us. We don't recognize our own growth, or that of our children when we are constantly in the presence of one another. It's only when we step back that we can see and identify. Such is our relationship to the earth. Gravity is such a constant theme, in our lives, that we don't even notice it. Like air, gravity facilitates all our actions and daily routines, but because most of us don't ever have a conscious experience of non-gravity, our kinship with earth is largely taken for granted. And yet, there are precious times in each of our lives, when we can remember, with our whole body if we so choose, a reverent and visceral connection with earth that is our cellular blueprint for every experience of connection we are blessed to have in our life.

I had an experience of this in 1993 while living on a long narrow peninsula in British Columbia flanked by the Georgia Strait and the Sunshine Coast Mountain range with my then partner, the Honorable Edward Chandler. A British misfit who somehow ended up in the temperate rainforest of western Canada, a "trustafarian" living off of his wealthy family's trust estate, Edward owned and stewarded ten forested acres in a rural community on a remote peninsula northeast of Vancouver.

From the moment I first visited him in his home, I was profoundly enchanted. Driving up his long, meandering driveway, completely overgrown with plant life, was like driving into the secret Bat Cave from my childhood memory of watching the popular TV program *Bat Man*. Once I emerged from the foliage, and passed a small A-frame cabin, I entered a clearing where a gorgeous house with multi-level decks appeared, a large swimming pond and mature trees on a clearing to the left, and a mostly treed and overgrown stand on my right. I followed the long drive and pulled in to park in front of what looked like a large workshop. Edward, I would learn, was a highly skilled wood craftsman, trained in England and impeccable in his art. He had invited me over to peel the bark off freshly felled cedar logs, which turned out to be a sensual delight that he somehow intuited I'd enjoy!

It would be a few years after that first visit in 1991, when Edward and I, having decided to have a family together, would find ourselves facing the limitation of my infertility, and trying desperately to reverse that prognosis on a spiritual level. Surrounded by a thriving community of alternative healers, artists, and environmental activists, it wasn't a surprise to us when we were approached by a Lakota medicine man, Joshua, to host a sweat lodge on our property for the use of community healing ceremonies. And thus began a yearlong dance with Native

American spiritual traditions and practices as Edward and I played the role of "keepers" of the lodge.

Patrick White Cloud, Joshua's elder, his teacher, offered me a hot coal peyote ceremony to help heal the issues that prevented me from conceiving, carrying, and birthing children. A hot coal ceremony consisted of sitting on the carpeted floor in a small room in our home with Patrick White Cloud as my Shamanic guide. A metal vessel lay before us. After ingesting the peyote sacrament, Ely, another apprentice of Patrick's would bring in hot coals for me to gaze into as I told my life story pertaining to my fertility and lack of it. Having learned at age sixteen that I lacked the estrogen production to support a growing fetus, and then at age twenty-two that I had no ovum or ovaries to conceive with, I'd been dancing with the prognosis of *infertile* for about fifteen years. Now, ready to have a family, I desperately wanted to prove that wrong so that I could conceive and carry my own child.

The ceremony must have lasted about two hours. During that time, my focus never strayed. With that focus I never registered an altered state that the peyote would have caused. I have very little recollection of the actual sharing that I did, but I do remember that I felt completely unaffected by the peyote.

When the ceremony ended, Uncle Pat, as he was affectionately known, gifted me with a rectangular-shaped crystal. It was now Edward's turn for ceremony. I left the small room and wandered outdoors. I strolled along the fenced pasture where the sheep and goats we shared our rural oasis with grazed, providing us with manure for our organic veggie garden. I gazed out over the wooden fence to the post and beam cedar-sided barn raised by Edward and friends. I began to register that I was indeed very much in an altered state and had been all throughout the ceremony. No longer hyper-focused as I was while staring into the hot coals, I could now detect the plant medicine affecting my conscious awareness. I chose to meander my way down the ravine to the sweat lodge where I knew there was a community sweat in progress. Walking past Edward's woodworking shop, through the alder grove, and down a trail took me to the lodge that sat at the convergence of two narrow creek beds.

There was no one around; the sweat had evidently already ended. I crawled into the lodge. She was still warm and the scent of cedar rose from the earth, permeating the blanketed walls suspended over the lodge's willow trunk skeleton. Lying on my belly, one leg bent, resting my head on my bent arm on the same side, my body surrendered its weight into the cushiony floor of the lodge strewn with cedar boughs. The warmth of this womb-like space, having just held the prayers of several of my sisters and brothers, took me in and cradled me lovingly. The sound of the creek lulled me into a gentle and safe place where I could journey with the sacred medicine and what was left of her plan for me. The cedar cushioned earth, pressed against my entire being allowed a mergence to take place that gave me a vivid taste of Ground and all she embodies.

The words earth and rest, have often been synonymous for me. Without a surrendered appreciation for the earth's presence, I don't think I have ever really known the experience of rest. As a distinctive quality in the essence of Ground, rest reminds us that allowing ourselves to be caught and held by our true mother, Earth, we find our oneness with all things. Acceptance of this oneness, a tangible felt Sense experience of this connection, is what Ground embraces. And though we are always in relationship with earth, it's only when we consciously intend it, that we are actually grounded.

Grounding in Home as a Place

Home can be thought of as grounding a sense of self in the world as we turn inward to our own heart for solace and meaning. Once we know this place within ourselves, we can then connect in a deep way to finding a sense of home in a geographical place by connecting to the spirit of that place.

One idea of home is a place where we've spent a lot of time. However, grounding a sense of home in an unfamiliar place by deeply embracing its essence through our felt Sense connection to the home within may be a new and expanded concept of home.

From my journal:

> "This place has opened its heart to me. I have no idea how long I'll be here, my mind wants to know and then I remind it that my heart is in charge, so instead of knowing it, I will be loving it, which will take me even deeper than knowing it, to connecting and meeting with it in oneness.
>
> The spirit of this place has offered itself to me for healing and discovery. Together we exist outside of physical time so that the history of this land and I are interwoven."

Home, as a physical place, awakens our awareness to the essence of that place. The events that happen in a place are not independent of her. In fact, when you look back at your experiences in important places, you may find that the place created the experience. In David Abram's book *The Spell of the Sensuous*, he writes:

> "A particular place is never, for an oral culture, just a passive or inert setting for the events that occurred there. It is an active participant in those occurrences, indeed it may even be thought to be the source, the

primary power that expresses itself through the various events that happen there.".

He goes on to say:

> "It is as though specific loci in the land release specific stories in those persons who travel them. Or as though, it is not the person who speaks, but rather the land that speaks through him as he journeys across it."

Grounding and Relationship

Grounding, in engineering terms, refers to circuiting energy into the earth. There is an implicit implication of relationship between energy and earth and possibly another "body" or energy conductor. "Relationship or relatedness cannot exist without communication or exchange between us and the other," writes Susan MacElroy in *Heart in the Wild*. And ". . . there is an intimate reciprocity to the senses; as we touch the bark of a tree, we feel the tree touching us . . ." writes David Abram in *The Spell of the Sensuous*.

These two statements together awaken us to how communication, necessary for relationship to take place, and grounding are interdependent and how the senses play a major role in communication and the reciprocity inherent in it. I believe that it's this reciprocity that gifts us with a grounded sense of the home within. In Vividly Woman we call this conscious dance of sensual reciprocity in nature, *Flirting with Nature*, which we explored in Chapter 2—Sensual Power.

With the intention to ground in the sacredness of a place, we can look for how the spirit of each place has a significant impact in the healing and awakening journey that took place there. By connecting the dots between the qualities of a place and the kinds of personal openings, insights, and connections you made there, you ground in that place. In my own experience I've seen how the heat of Mexico warmed my heart, how vast desert landscapes gave me room to feel, and how the winding roads of Cortes Island led pathways into my soul. Connecting the quality of a place to the quality of my inner journey while there, grounds me in the more than human world of nature and allows me to see my reflection in her.

Sacredness of Place Exercise

1. Make a list of the places that have been important to you over your life. Places you've lived or visited where you felt a sense of homecoming and comfort.
2. One by one, go through this list and add descriptive qualities of each place.
3. One by one, add insights of what you learned, created or healed while you were in each place.
4. Notice the relationships between the qualities of each place and what your experience was there.

Embodying Ground

As an infant you learned how to move through space by leveraging your body against and away from the earth. You started by creeping, belly to belly against the earth, reaching out to pull yourself along the ground. Eventually, you pushed yourself away from her to give yourself more ease of motion, and instinctively learned how to push off, one knee and hand in cross-crawl to give you even greater ease of locomotion. No one taught you this; it came naturally and instinctively. When you were able to stand, you used gravity in order to move into upright stance. As your walking became second nature, you gradually became less and less dependent on the earth to move you, and more and more reliant on the function of your own body.

Walking became a habit supported by the ability and ease to flex the hip joint instead of pressing your foot against the earth to push off by leveraging earth's solidity. This gradual distance from the earth as a source of our ability to move is a statement in our eventual distance and objectification of her as separate from us, instead of connected as one with her. If you want to revisit the experience of embodying earth in each step, simply experiment with pressing the earth away with each foot as you extend your ankle joint instead of flexing your hip. I call this way of walking the sexy earth walk. One of my workshop participants claimed that nature flirted with her a lot more when she walked this way through the forest!

Light and Shadow

The ability to release into and resource gravity to leverage one's self is a light expression of Ground. We use the earth in order to stabilize and orient ourselves. That's grounding. Ground brings us from the energetic conceptual quality of Sense into tangible form on the physical plane. Where Sense planted the seed, Ground in its light aspect guides us to map out a step-by-step plan that will ultimately require implementation in order to grow that seed into a mature plant.

Witness consciousness is a light dimension of Ground that is the balanced state of being able to be conscious of dynamics that stem from the stories we weave. When we adopt an objective awareness, a perch from where we can see and still remain centered, we are grounded. This is an important step in coming into mastery of one's Emotional Power that we explored in Chapter 3: The ability to see and access the full spectrum of our emotions, but not be at the mercy of their story and the power to pick and choose what is most appropriate to express, when, and where.

I am an advocate for feeling and expressing anger, but I believe that it's irresponsible and immature to assume that others should have to witness it unless they have consented. At a workshop I attended years ago the leader said, "The expression of anger is like going to the bathroom. You don't assume that anyone else wants to be there with you, so the same goes for the expression of rage."

This came back to me when I was just getting Vividly Woman going and I was collaborating on an event with a friend of mine. I was living in Mexico at the time and phone and Internet were very sketchy. Ann got really angry with me and raged at me over the phone because she hadn't been able to reach me. I was shocked by the blame and anger, but most of all the assumption she made that it was all right to unload it all on me. I told her that I wasn't open to being dumped on that way. Her belief was that I should be available for whatever she was feeling and be able to receive it. Our differing perspectives obviously caused the ending of our collaboration and sadly our friendship. Though I still consider her a cherished sister whom I hope to one day reconcile with, I still feel grounded in my right to choose what I will be a witness to and to honor my boundaries.

When we attach to the earth beyond what is reasonable, not allowing our self to take the necessary next steps, remain stuck in the past or certain dogmatic ideas, we're in the shadow side of Ground. The inability to ebb and flow, to bend with the tides and the winds, causes us to snap and break instead of go with the flow. Attached to a story, unwilling to embrace the freedom of truth, is the dark side of Ground.

I inherited an overly controlling nature from my mother. Whether it was the instability in her early life, as a foster child of the holocaust, or because her own mother was overly controlling while her father was a more passive character, Mum walked in the world in a very directive way that pre-empted most events and activities, killing spontaneity and the ability to adapt to uncertain life situations. After a two-and-a-half year battle with lung cancer, Mum died in the hospital in Montreal just a couple of days before a weeklong retreat I was hosting in Mexico. Fifteen women were on their way down to spend a week in paradise diving into their own Embodied Goddess Awakening. Fortunately, anticipating the possibility of having to leave the retreat because of my mother's condition, I'd documented all the retreat practices and processes so that my trained apprentices could take over.

Would I have been ready to hand over the reigns were I not forced to? No, I don't think my own controlling nature would have let me do that. However, with little other choice because my priority was to be with my family, I was asked to step out of the controlling nature I had inherited from my mother in order to be in my highest integrity and be at her funeral with my family. My mother's last gift to me was to break the cycle of control that I had learned from her. Among the many blessings of what at first seemed like poor timing, was that it took my business to the next level, grew my level of trust in my apprentices, now graduated to facilitator status, which is ultimately what has allowed me to grow Vividly Woman Embodied Leader Training.

Getting stuck in your story is another shadow aspect of Ground. Being able to resource the power of Mobilize, the 3rd texture of Vividly Woman that follows Ground, to move out of the story and its limiting beliefs facilitates freedom and healing. Often we walk around wearing our stories on our sleeve. We identify with the difficult times we've gone through and let everyone know how much we suffer because of it. We have grounded so deeply in this story that we are lost without it.

Is there a default identity that you fall back on to elicit a reaction from the people you spend time with or when you meet new acquaintances? Do you gravitate toward sharing things about yourself that are safe, shocking, self-victimizing or intriguing rather than being yourself and risking genuine intimacy? These are some of the indicators that story is active in your life and relationships.

Obsessive grounding in story is the antithesis of living in your body. Story is all about what's happening in your head. Truth is what lives in your body, and if you pay attention to it, honor and respect it, your body will be healthy and fit. If you consistently ignore your body, and what it's saying to you in order to live in the story of your mind, your body's truth will become more and more disruptive in an attempt to get your attention. That's what we call disease.

Ground Goddess

Demeter is the goddess who most embodies Ground. "[Demeter] taught mankind the art of sowing and ploughing so they could end their nomadic existence. As such, Demeter was also the goddess of planned society," writes Micha F. Lindemans in *Encyclopedia Mythica*.

Demeter is known to be the mother of Persephone, the Eternal Maiden Goddess. Together, they represent the mother daughter bond that ties women together in such a rich and profound way. Their close relationship is what generated the creation of the seasons that we know on Earth.

The Greek legend of Persephone tells us that one day while the two were out sowing their seeds in wild flower meadows, frolicking about doing their Goddess Earth Mother/daughter thing, Persephone went missing. Try as she might, Demeter wasn't able to find her. Later, we learn that Persephone was snatched into the underworld by Hades himself, King of the Underworld, and is being held prisoner there in the hopes that she will become his pride and underworld queen.

There are many versions of this tale, but what they all amount to is that Persephone, while resisting any of his tempting offers to be seduced into union with Hades, ultimately succumbs to his seductions only when she realizes she's finally free to leave. In her penultimate moment of captivity, as she is about to take the freedom she is offered, she accepts his offer of three pomegranate seeds. Her acceptance of his gift means that she must forever after spend half the year with Hades as Queen of the Underworld, and the other half with her mother on the Earth. When she is gone, Demeter creates winter on Earth as her expression of sorrow for missing her beloved daughter.

What does this have to do with grounding? Well first of all, as we know Demeter is the Earth Mother Goddess. She is an icon of all things Earth. Furthermore, we see the profound element of relationship in her story and how her daughter chose to ground her identity beyond that of Maiden, into the realm of queen, something she must have unconsciously struggled to attain in the dynamic between her and the all-encompassing Mother archetype that her mother embodied.

What we choose to ground ourselves in and around speaks volumes about our life and our journey. The point is that we do have a choice. Grounding is a conscious action, and as women we can choose what we are grounding ourselves in and about. Until we ask ourselves the question, *what grounds me?* It's hard to know the truth beneath the roles and externally imposed expectations and needs that we are living and dancing out of habit instead of authentic preference.

So ask yourself this question: What is it that Grounds You?

Ground Icon

One paragon of Ground recognized in our culture is Margaret Thatcher. Steadfast and unwavering in her role as British Prime Minister, she is known as the Iron Lady.

Other icons of Ground we acknowledge are Mother Teresa, Sacajawea, and Queen Noor of Jordan.

Ground at Work

In sense we discovered the value of aligning energetically with our desired outcome. Ground is the next and essential stage in order to generate results on the physical plane, moving from energy to form.

In Ground, we apply the wisdom of a tangible, step-by-step plan that encourages momentum and provides direction. Without the Ground stage in your work, too much is left to chance, mood, the weather, and the many surprises that occur along the road. Even with a plan in place you have to be prepared to re-evaluate and change course. However the plan keeps you on target so that even though the route may (and likely will) change, you always have your destination in view.

A marketing calendar that charts out the timelines for your projects, a business plan that provides an overview for your goals, documenting logistics and protocols are all Grounding strategies. They not only help you to stay on track, they make it way easier to enroll the support of others in your vision.

Ground in Relationship to the Textures

The key word for Ground in relationship to the other textures is *presence*. Authentic presence with the home within us gives a profound and tangible connection to this quality of connection with our body temple. A woman's experience of the home within herself is made more vivid and safe by the presence that ground inspires.

Chapter 6 Summary: Ground

~ We ground to give ourselves a sense of landing at home within ourselves, in relationship to the physical body that is our temple. Orienting oneself in the home within is the ultimate gift of Ground.

~ Grounding a sense of home in an unfamiliar place by deeply embracing its essence through our felt Sense connection to the home within may be a new and expanded concept of home.

~ Connecting the quality of a place to the quality of my inner journey while there, grounds me in the more than human world of nature and allows me to see my reflection in her.

~ Ground brings the conceptual quality of Sense to the tangible dimension of form.

~ Getting stuck in your story is a shadow aspect of Ground.

~ When we adopt an objective awareness, a perch from where we can see and still remain centered, then we are grounded.

~ The keyword for Ground is *presence*.

**To arouse your embodied power,
visit our "Ground" stimulators at**

www.VividlyWoman.com

"You will find meaning in life only if you create it. It is a poetry to be composed. It is a song to be sung. It is a dance to be danced..."
~ Osho

CHAPTER 7

Mobilize

Meaning that Motivates and Ignites Your Life

The awareness of Sense and the presence of Ground set the stage for meaning, the essence of the third texture of Vividly Woman: Mobilize. For women, devotion to what is truly meaningful in our lives is essential for a life richly lived. As the word implies, Mobilize is about moving into action, but from a place of authentic meaning.

When I was growing up I learned that if you were going to get somewhere in life, you had to be committed. Life was about working hard and proving your worth. Even at the expense of your life. I watched my father's stressful, high blood pressure lifestyle climbing the corporate ladder cause him to have a heart attack and die at age forty-nine.

'You don't get anywhere for nothing, there's no free ride, and if you don't choose a path, commit to it, and follow through on that commitment you'll never amount to anything," were typical beliefs and values that surrounded me.

Sound familiar? Though attitudes and trends change with time, this one doesn't seem to change. We are still telling our children to find a focus and be willing to stick with it come rain or shine.

I personally don't operate by commitment. Commitment is about sticking it out, proving my word, seeing it through, in spite of what I truly believe, want or need, just because I said I would, because I committed. Commitment is about the past, not about the present. It's about something I said, signed or paid for that I'm condemned to complete or consume even if it kills me!

Devotion, on the other hand is entirely about the present moment. I'm not sure of the exact moment or event that precipitated me discovering the concept of devotion, but it happened around the time that I found my body; I mean *really* found my body. I knew I had a body all along of course, I even trained as a dancer for many years, performing and competing rigorously, but it wasn't until I discovered the pleasure of my body (and I don't mean sexual pleasure although that is certainly a pleasurable perk of having a body), that I discovered the joy of paying attention to what my heart and soul really pine for, now in this moment, and the next and the next.

What started out as dance training, became a profound vehicle for self-discovery. Dance, which I had an obvious aptitude for from an early age, had always been something I was attracted to, but when my commitment to my teacher to train as intensely as I could to win ribbons became more important than my devotion to my own well-being (which meant having fun and doing what other kids do, play) I lost interest and dropped out of the all-encompassing, driving need to accomplish something, to achieve perfection, to please my teacher. Instead I discovered, that as much as I loved to dance, I loved listening to my greater calling, which was to have fun, be with other kids, and do stuff just for the sake of doing stuff, in other words, just be a kid!

Now, as an adult, I still love to play, I love to follow my creative intuition, I love to let my heart decide based on what I honestly feel in each moment. I call that living devotion. Is it possible to ever complete a project this way, achieve a sense of fulfillment, and realize a dream? I'm thrilled to testify that not only is devotion effective at generating all of the above; it actually has a deeper impact for the reasons that follow.

Devotion is about sensing inwardly to our own alive and pulsing animal nature in each moment. The muscle and lifeblood of devotion is current real life magic that ignites your flame, that makes you laugh, that inspires you to dream.

In a linear, more masculine, goal-oriented context, Mobilize is about moving into action to get from point a to point b. Without action, it's unlikely that there will be any movement. In a sculptural, feminine context, Mobilize is about identifying the meaning that motivates action. Without meaning, there is no point in taking action, because you won't be able to sustain that action, or if you do, it will be at the expense of your soul's true calling. I've seen many cases of chronic depression, anxiety, and spiritual death caused by this unhealthy recipe.

 Meaning sustains action so that you achieve more with less effort.

Devotion and meaning are somewhat synonymous. If you fill your life with things and people that are genuinely meaningful to you, you'll likely have a stronger sense of devotion to those things and people and it will seem like much less of a strain to do the things that are required to keep those relationships alive. The opposite is true as well. Less meaning means more drudgery. It's the difference, in other words, between living a vivid Technicolor existence or one in multiple shades of gray.

Finding Meaning

But what do you do with all the mundane daily responsibilities that don't inherently feel attractive to you, like taking out the garbage, making the kids their lunch day after day, or paying the bills? For those things and people that you might not actually choose given the option, but are necessary for functioning in your world, your task is to choose to find meaning in doing them, or don't bother! Essentially you have two choices. Choose to do things that have meaning, or choose to find meaning in the things that you do. The power to choose is something we cannot, as women living with the means and the opportunity that we have, ignore. It is precisely because we can choose, that we must, and in so doing, create meaningful, rich lives for ourselves.

When you look carefully, it's easy to find the meaning in those things that feel like chores. Taking out the garbage for instance is meaningful because it means that you have the wealth to acquire goods that will make your life easier, keep you fed, and run your home. Its obvious why it's meaningful to make lunch for your kids, and paying the bills means you have access to the things that serve your ease and comfort, a luxury not to be taken for granted.

But there may be even deeper meaning in the menial chores that you avoid. Christina shared her big aha from having to unclog a drain:

"Recently, I noticed the drain in my bathroom sink was clogged. I looked down the drain. It was very dark and sort of slimy. It looked like a job for my husband, but he was unavailable, so I found some tweezers and dug in.

What I pulled out was downright nasty. Chunks of gooey ooze that used to be nice things like soap, toothpaste, and hair. Sludge would be a great way to describe it. I really wished my husband could do this job so I didn't have to be exposed to such grossness. Then I had a change of heart. I remembered the Vividly Woman practice of being able to find the meaning in any task. So I started thinking about the job I was doing and once I did, it became rewarding. It actually felt really good to pull out those chunks of yuck.

On a superficial level, the meaning in this job was that we would soon have a functional drain again. I was also doing something that expressed my love for my family. More than that, I was able to find meaning by comparing the drain cleaning to my own personal growth experience. It became the perfect metaphor.

It took a fairly significant event for me to notice that all was not well under the sink. I didn't notice until the drain was almost completely clogged. Likewise, it took significant signs in my life to realize that not all was well under my happy exterior. In one shocking moment of personal growth, I discovered that I had mountains of repressed anger buried deep within me. They were choking off my ability to experience emotion.

This experience with my clogged drain helped me to realize that when my body is clogged with residue from unfelt emotions, it's almost impossible to find my higher self. When I allow those emotions to move through me and when I can be the master of those emotions, rather than the victim, my access to my spirit is free to flow."

> ### *Discovering Meaning Practice*
>
> 1. Make a list of those things you don't like to have to do
> 2. Beside each item write why it's meaningful for you to do it
> 3. When you go to do each of the things on your list, keep its meaning in your awareness

Sometimes, excavating meaning has nothing to do with day-to-day chores and doesn't require much digging at all. The writing, so to speak, is on the wall, and motivates actions you've been avoiding. That's how Mobilize played a part in the dance of my infertility and my longing to be a mother.

It happened when all of the spiritual efforts to heal my infertility failed. It was then that Edward and I decided to adopt. We met with the social worker, completed our home study, and learned the ropes about open adoption. After signing, sealing, and sending our home study to 125 doctors in Canada, a friend asked us to adopt her baby due to be born in five months. This would be her second, and she didn't feel that she and the father could support another child. Of course, we were hesitant at first, and we sent her to counselors and social workers to make sure she had made a clear and true decision. She maintained her position; she wanted to give us her child. Mutual friends who were mothers thought she was crazy, and members of my family warned me not to get too excited. My husband was fairly nonchalant about it. I was torn as to what was the right course, but in the end I chose to believe this child was meant to be ours. I stepped in to psychically nurture the growing fetus whose mother was preparing to let him go. What else could I do? This child needed a mother to love him while in the womb—someone who was ready to receive him when the time came. It was my honor to be called on to care for this baby as best I could during those five months of gestation.

Then, the bubble burst. Two weeks before the due date, our friend changed her mind. I was stunned and sorrowful, but it wasn't until she gave birth that I actually felt my body's grief, as if I had given birth myself and had given up the baby. A roar and an ache erupted from within me. My husband remained indifferent and unable to empathize with my pain and loss. For me, there was profound meaning in his emotional distance that I could no longer ignore. This event expanded a wedge already present between us that would eventually break us apart.

As you can see finding meaning requires attention to what you're devoted to. Sometimes you also need a good helping of courage to see true meaning because it could mean having to make changes that will upset the current trajectory of your life.

Moving to Mobilize

In a book on embodiment, discussing the value of moving, dancing, shaking, etc. would be obvious. And while our path of embodied awakening does indeed include a healthy dose of each of the above, they are not limited exclusively to the texture of Mobilize. They do give us access to a quick, easy, and sensual way of getting energy moving when action is required, shifting stagnant energy that is detrimental to an outcome or inner state, and of attaining states of spiritual ecstasy and meaning all very related to Mobilize. In Chapter 14 you'll read about how to bring dance and movement into each element of the Vividly Woman Solar System.

Dance as a path to ecstasy has been used since the beginning of time. Indigenous people used it as prayer to communicate with their spirit gods. Whether as a rite of passage, a healing ceremony or a sacred celebration, dance was a big part of traditional ritual. The Haitians are known for their ecstatic voodoo trance dance ceremonies. The Maoris from New Zealand are known for their Haka war dance. The Sufis have their whirling dervish dance. "Peoples of every society and of every era have addressed the sacred through the mediums of music and dance," writes Ezra Gardner Rust, author of *The Music and Dance of the World's Religions*.

While dance has been practiced and enjoyed by both men and women through history, it holds a special place in the evolution of goddess consciousness and therefore all women. "The image of the Goddess is an important symbol for women as we seek out our sacred dance heritage. Knowing about the priestess and understanding her unique role, however, is essential because the priestess is a real, historical woman—a woman we can identify with. Through the priestess and her sacred dances, we learn that women were once central to religious and spiritual practices and that women had their own rites—their own symbols and liturgies—separate from those of men," writes Iris J. Stewart in her beautiful book *Sacred Woman, Sacred Dance*.

Dance has been a profound vehicle for healing, awakening, and creative fulfillment in my life. Though I learned dance as a child, and trained rigorously as I mentioned above, it wasn't until my father had a heart attack on the dance floor, and then died, that I feel I actually started dancing. It was then that I took to dancing as healing for my grief, which gave birth to dancing as spiritual practice in later years.

While there were a lot of drugs and alcohol involved in dancing my grief, dance became a refuge where I could disappear and dive deep into the mystery of life and death that had just been introduced to me. Shocked to the core by the reality of suddenly losing my father, I was keenly awoken to the awareness that I only really understood and had conscious access to a limited portion of reality. The altered state that I visited through dance, albeit chemically induced, became an intriguing adventure that brought me closer to making sense of the tenuous nature of our existence. Later, I would come to understand this to be what's known as a *numinous* or mystical experience that profoundly altered my life.

The portal of dancing to process my grief, brought me to a place of profound intimacy with myself. This place of connection was a safe and pain free place. There was no sense of abandonment, loss, confusion, or pain associated with Dad's passing. I was one with all of life and this was a state where I felt connected to my father. Later, without drugs or alcohol, I discovered that other overriding feelings and judgments that threatened my self-worth and self-esteem were also suspended in this euphoric dance state. The deeper meaning of my life, and all life became accessible to me through this practice. This brought peace, joy, and fulfillment that I craved more of and would come to design my life around.

Light and Shadow

Moving into action is essential for any dream to become a reality. You have to be willing to exert some energy, walk your talk, and dance the next step. Taking those first few steps are often the most difficult, the most intimidating, but once a dream is set in motion through your honest and devoted effort, it's amazing how momentum can soon almost completely take over. As long as you are passionately aligned with your outcome, action can often become second nature and gravitational.

With a clear plan in place, action has direction, it has purpose, and each action step will enhance the steps that came before. This is the light, or positive side of Mobilize.

It's great to be able to actually do what you say you are going to. You establish trust in others and in yourself. Integrity is strengthened and you become a person that others can rely on and turn to.

However, if you are the sort of person who is always in action mode, constantly launching new projects, moving forward on all or most visionary possibilities that you come up with, you are likely living on the shadow side of Mobilize and sooner, likely rather than later, you will burn out from exhaustion.

The dark side of Mobilize is Mobilize without a healthy dose of Ground to stabilize and give you the tools to discern what is most efficient and realistic as you move forward. The combination of Mobilize and Ground is what we'll explore in Chapter 8—Harness.

I used to be a very Mobilize sort of person. I was always coming up with amazing new ideas. Without thinking them through, I would get excited about the possibilities and launch into the actions that would get me there.

People were always commenting about how much I had going on. It was baffling to understand how I could manage so many balls in the air at one time. While I was loving everything I was doing, and feeling incredibly and creatively on fire, at a certain point I looked at the tangible results I was accomplishing, and when I saw that the outcomes were not living up to my initial intentions, my energy started to wane until I did start to see that I had diluted my focus and available energy so much that everything I was doing was suffering.

I remember taking a walk with one of my staff members, Shona, between sessions at a Vividly Woman event. I was going through some major emotional processing because my mother had been diagnosed with lung cancer. Shona, my dear sister for almost twenty years, was helping me to express and heal some of the grief I was carrying at having to let go of my mum in the near future. For some reason the topic of how busy I was came up. I guess because it was going to get in the way of me spending time with my mother. And also because as I acknowledged the sorrow of knowing that my mother would pass soon, I became conscious of how much I was doing in order to prove myself to her, to feel like a success in my mother's eyes. I promised Shona that I wouldn't launch any more new projects for at least a year to create the space that would allow me to devote myself to being with my mother instead of proving my worth to her. Having the time and space to choose that, over my work, is what true success felt like.

Over the next year, as my existing projects were winding down, I started to notice myself feeling kind of un-inspired, no longer on fire. I had practiced saying no a lot, turning down invitations to collaborate or facilitate. The well started to feel dried up in my business life, and Vividly Woman, though still alive and vital, was experiencing somewhat of a lull with the economy tanked and the personal development and live event industry suffering. As is typical for me and the low self-esteem cast of characters that reside in my psyche, I started to blame myself and the worth of my service. "Nobody wants what I have to offer, what I've poured my heart and soul into, etc." Then, fortunately I remembered that walk in the woods with Shona. I remembered that I had made a promise not to take on any new projects so that I could devote more free time to my mother. And that is exactly why things were slowing down, just as I had intended!

Emotional Power

Mobilize predominantly corresponds to Emotional Power in the VW Solar System. There are two types of meaning, meaning of the head, and meaning of the heart. In the VW Training we are mainly concerned with meaning of the heart. We have all had sufficient training in meaning of the head. If you've been through the school system, you have spent countless hours learning how to think, reason, and solve problems using your cognitive abilities. These are important faculties to develop, unfortunately though, the school system doesn't balance things out so that while you are growing in your rational skills you are simultaneously cultivating your heart expansion and knowing that to be important too. In Chapter 4—Emotional Power, we looked at why Emotional Power is so essential for women. Mobilize is the texture that has been most misunderstood and abused so that doing is more important than being. As a result, we lost sight of why we do the things we do, and the doing of stuff became more important than the why we are doing them in the first place. Keeping busy, distracting ourselves, always needing external stimulation, these are symptoms of a culture that has evolved on the shadow side of Mobilize.

It is said that separation is about the mind while union is about the heart. Heart meaning brings together what is most life sustaining: love and purpose. As we shall see in the next chapter, Harness, Mobilize and meaning are vital aspects of being able to sustain actions in order to bring about real life, genuinely fulfilling results.

 Meaning and creativity mutually nourish each other and help us to process difficult emotions.

Creativity is a powerful dimension of Mobilize. As we become more heart centered and motivated by what most touches and moves us at an emotional level, we are profoundly inspired to share that aliveness at a creative level. While I've seen repressed emotion be a phenomenal creative catalyst, it is far more fulfilling and life-sustaining to be able to fuel your creative endeavors while also being able to express, clear, and share oneself emotionally. And the beautiful part is that we can have both. While I've met several artistic people who clearly pour their vulnerability exclusively into their craft, I have never met an emotionally rich and mature individual who didn't exude an enormous creative aura. They seem to go hand in hand, and the result is very inspiring.

The tears and the laughter that we experience together in sacred circle are a potent catalyst for creativity. Letting the emotions flow can give enormous freedom to what was once withheld and kept private for fear of being seen, judged, and rejected. Once you've let yourself be seen in one context, it's far easier to let yourself be seen in other ways as well.

I've always found it easy to dance transparently. For some reason, I enter into an almost hypnotic state in relationship to music, my environment, my body, and with my inner world. Being seen or witnessed when I am immersed in this deep self-expression carries no charge or fear for me. Singing on the other hand, and even speaking at one time, was terrifying for me. Singing exposed me in a way I couldn't bear risking. I literally felt like I was standing naked. I decided to devote myself to moving beyond my fears and anxiety around my voice. The first thing my singing coach did was to encourage me to choose a song that held emotional meaning for me. I had come wanting to sing like Queen Latifah because I liked the sound of her voice, but Deborah, my coach, asked me to name a recording artist who moved me emotionally. Karen Carpenter immediately came to mind. I've always been touched by her story around her body image issues and her anorexia that were the cause of her tragic death. We started our work together with a Karen Carpenter song that captured the essence of what I was going through emotionally at that time in my life, which was courting my mother in her last months. I chose the song "We've only just begun," because in spite of the heartache and fear of her imminent passing, I also implicitly knew that our connection would continue beyond my mother's lifetime. I intuitively knew that my mother's passing was not only an ending, but also the meaningful beginning of a new dimension of our relationship. I sang the lyrics "So much in life ahead, we'll find a place where there's room to grow," trusting the gifts inherent in the mystery that is the cycle of life. Now, almost two years since my mother's transition, our connection has indeed deepened with time and the experience of resourcing our relationship on a different plane. That doesn't mean I don't ever feel sadness about her passing. It just means that sadness is only one of lots of different feelings I have in relationship with my mother.

Mobilize Icons

Some noteworthy Mobilize icons are Florence Nightingale, Zainab Salbi, founder of Women for Women International, and Gloria Steinem. All these women have broken new ground through their tenacious vision for meaning, justice and change.

Goddess

One of the Goddesses that most brings the essence of Mobilize into our personal mythology is Tara. A Buddhist Goddess, Tara is said to have two aspects. Her white aspect is devoted to wisdom and purity of heart, and her green aspect is devoted to action. Together, these two aspects of Tara are thought of as a savioress. She is known for her love and desire to save being stronger than a mother's love for her children. Tara is a shining symbol of heart meaning in action.

Mobilize in Business

I've always been fascinated by marketing—the art of motivating people to invest in what we offer. Marketing is a vital aspect of your business and your business plan. *Start with Why*, a book and a marketing model written by Simon Sinek, is a great example of the Mobilize texture applied to business. *Start with Why* teaches us that even before "how" and "what," we need to have and communicate a clear and passionate "why" in order to be able to inspire others to want what we've got. In other words, the meaning of a product—it's value—is more vital than the delivery or the quality of that product or service. The Mobilize texture as it applies to business reminds us that the heart of our service is the essence of our success, supporting the emerging feminine business paradigm.

Mobilize in Relation to the Textures

The key word for Mobilize in relationship to the other textures is *meaning*. Meaning brings us into intimate communion with the unpredictable and mysterious journey home and with each of the steps that take us there. A woman's devotion to her journey home is sustained and deepened by the meaning that Mobilize inspires.

Chapter 7 Summary: Mobilize

~ Commitment is based on the past. Devotion is about sensing inwardly to our own alive and pulsing animal nature in each present moment.

~ Mobilize is about moving into action, but from a place of authentic meaning.

~ Choose to do things that have meaning, or choose to find meaning in the things that you do.

~ Moving our body gives us access to a quick, easy, and sensual way of getting energy moving when action is required. This shifting of stagnant energy can help us to achieve an outcome, encourage an inner state and attain states of spiritual ecstasy and meaning.

~ As long as you are passionately aligned with your outcome, action can become second nature and gravitational.

~ Heart meaning brings together what is most life sustaining: love and purpose.

~ Mobilize and meaning are vital aspects of being able to sustain actions in order to bring about real life, genuinely fulfilling results.

~ The Mobilize texture as it applies to business reminds us that the heart of our service, the *why*, is the essence of our success, supporting the immerging feminine business paradigm.

~ The keyword for Mobilize is *meaning*.

**To arouse your embodied power,
visit our "Mobilize" stimulators at**

www.VividlyWoman.com

> *"Inner marriage- the new masculine with the new feminine in divine embrace."*
> –Marion Woodman

CHAPTER 8

Harness

Sustain Expansion: Make More Out of Less

In the last two chapters we learned the value of Ground and the heart and soul of Mobilize. Now we'll put these two textures together to enclose (Ground) energy in motion (Mobilize) to encourage energy expansion. Our felt Sense experience of this dance is what we call, Harness, the fourth texture of Vividly Woman. We use the word Harness to refer to containing or capturing something. As it applies to the five textures of Vividly Woman, Harness is the act of containing energy in order to expand it. Based on the concept that when we enclose or block energy it naturally grows its force and power, Harness is a texture that is vital for our ability to expand and empower ourselves in just about every area of our lives. Money, sex, and health are just a few of the areas that thrive with the practice of Harness.

When we apply Harness to Emotional Power as we explored in Chapter 3, we see that harnessing emotions is different than suppressing emotions. When you suppress your feelings, trying not to feel or express them, you feel contracted, deadened, and disempowered. When you harness your emotions, choosing when to fully feel and express them, you feel expanded, conscious, and creatively empowered.

We see examples of the wisdom of Harness in our dance with nature all around us. The way a dam is used to harness water, creating hydroelectric power, or the way a sail is used to harness wind, to propel a boat.

From your own life Harness likely plays a major role in your relationship to money. You earn money. If all you do is spend it, you have to go and earn some more. If, on the other hand you invest it and spend the interest, you're harnessing your money in order to work more efficiently, leveraging your past efforts so that you can enjoy your results instead of having to always recreate them. Harnessing energy is a mature and wise use of your resources.

Let's look at body weight, an issue that many women can relate to. Here's a common scenario that might twig your own memory.

You've spent the last few months paying close attention to your diet and exercise regimen. You've managed to happily release several extra pounds and you're feeling great. Let's say you've even reached your goal weight. You celebrate with friends and go out for a delicious rich French meal, and you even treat yourself to a chocolate éclair for dessert, after all this is a very renowned French restaurant, everything is home made, and the pastry chef trained at Cordon Bleu and has won several culinary awards. It would be crazy not to indulge.

And you can clearly afford to. You've reached your goal by honoring your devotion to your ideal weight and the health of your beautiful temple. Your friends celebrate with you, and you even drink a little more wine than usual. It turns out to be a beautiful evening, everyone shares and laughs and you feel blessed to have dear friends who are there to share important milestones in your life.

The next day, you feel a little bloated, a little groggy, but it's Sunday so you can kick back, not worry about work or anything but yourself. Around noon you start feeling peckish and instead of reaching for a choice of one of the low calorie breakfasts you've been savoring (or convincing yourself that you're savoring) these last few months, you decide you deserve some pancakes. It's been four months without pancakes and bacon, and hell you can afford them. The syrup is of course a natural accompaniment, and even a latte to help wash it all down. You skip lunch because breakfast was so late, but by dinnertime you've already made a mental list of all the things you didn't eat for four months and you are hankering for a four-cheese pizza at Luigi's Pizzeria and the tiramisu that you used to share with an old lover.

Okay, maybe this is a bit of an exaggeration, or maybe not. But it is a clear illustration of a very unharnessed, inefficient relationship to energy. You've worked hard and respected your body for all those months, now only to abandon all reason. Naturally, you start to gain the weight back. You keep telling yourself you'll start back on the diet again, but one day leads into the next and before you know it you've gained back six of the thirty you lost. Oops!!!!

The harnessed version of this story is that you enjoyed a wonderful dinner out with dear friends celebrating (this is the next texture by the way, Express) and the morning after, you wake up with a smile, savoring the way you are going to take good care of yourself and continue conscious eating practices that allow you to indulge the way you did last night once every week or two. You don't have to make up for the ways you denied yourself, because the last four months weren't about denial, they were about honoring, and that is the energy you want to harness.

With this attitude and habit of maintenance you easily maintain your ideal weight and take this mastery of the texture of Harness into other important areas of your life like finances, sexuality, relationship, and exercise.

Does the unharnessed version of the story sound familiar to you? I know it does for me. I can remember a few times in my own life when I behaved in a similar way to what I described above.

When I was around eighteen, I was put on hormone replacement therapy because I wasn't menstruating naturally and I had low estrogen production in my body. My doctor was concerned about the density of my bones and insisted that estrogen replacement was essential. At the time, the only option was the low dose birth control pill. My mother agreed that for the health of my skeleton, and so that I would have monthly periods like all my friends, synthetic hormone therapy was a wise choice.

After about two months on those pills and patches, I had gained twenty lbs. For a woman of 5' 4" and small boned, that was a lot of weight. After gasping at the numbers on the scale, I quickly got myself to a weight loss clinic where I had to weigh in five days a week. In six weeks I had lost the weight, I felt like myself again, and had learned some great recipes that I loved preparing and eating. Mm . . . I can still remember the low fat pineapple bran muffins, the poached chicken breast with tomatoes, and my morning breakfast of cottage cheese mixed with apricot jam and Special K!

Everything was going great, until a guy I had a crazy crush on finally asked me on a date. We had a wild evening together at my place, my mother was away at her boyfriend's, and Danny ended up staying the night.

Everything I had longed for was coming true. He did love me after all. We had passionate (alcohol intoxicated) sex all evening, but when we awoke in the morning it was kind of uncomfortable and I could tell that when he left without breakfast, this was not about love, it was just a wild sexual encounter. I was pretty hung over from the night before, and my way of dealing with a hangover was always to have a big breakfast to ground me.

I specifically remember going into the bread drawer and taking out the darn bag of pita bread I had denied myself all those months, and proceeding to make myself an indulgent, over the top breakfast of champions to make up for and repress the feelings of rejection and self-betrayal that threatened to make their way to the surface. I called a friend to brag about my juicy night in the sack with my sexy crush, never daring to share how crushed I really was by being used and then dumped. One breakfast led into the next meal and the next and the next, until I had gained back part of the weight. This experience, and others like it helped me develop a pattern of using food to avoid feeling my shame, heartbreak, low self-esteem, and loneliness.

I share this story to illustrate how we sabotage ourselves when we don't look honestly and aren't willing to feel the truth of our feelings. Suppressing our feelings, you may recall from Chapter 3—Emotional Power, turns them into shadow material, that comes back to bite us in the butt and act out in all kinds of destructive ways.

Addiction and Self-Sabotage

Speaking of self-destruction, addiction, the abusive use of substances to sabotage our expansion, is one of the most rampant epidemics in our culture. Addiction is literally the subconscious attempt to leak the energy that harnessing has managed to accumulate.

If you're able to sense inwardly and pay attention to the sensations of addiction, the body's language for discomfort and stress around risking expansion and all the life altering results that come with it, you'll find that your body is speaking to you quite clearly before you take that puff, down that drink, or spend that money you vowed never to use without consent of your partner or wise woman counsel or business advisory board.

If you're anything like me, your body is probably starting to shake a little, there's a tremble in your arms and belly, you can't sit still, and there's a bleeding sensation in your throat. If you listen and devote yourself to lovingly attending to and breathing with the sensations, you'll find that you can do just that without taking any next steps to quell or change them as you have in the past, which is why you have an addiction.

If on the other hand you ignore those cues, literally pretend you don't even notice them, and on some level you don't, you go right for the thing that you know in the past has helped to stop the trembling, the giddiness, the fear, the anxiety. If you drown those sensations out enough with whatever habit or substance of preference you can get your hands on, you might even be able to sleep through the night, go to work, or sit through your daughter's piano recital without having a panic attack. But at what cost to you and those you love? That is the dance of addiction.

The nervous energy, that takes place at the edge of your energy container, is spirit's way of telling you that growth and expansion are imminent. And with that, other things in your life will likely change. With your expanded power and authentic self-worth, your husband will need to learn how to make love to you the way you really like it, your kids will have to settle for one sleepover a week so that you can get some much needed rest, your clients will have to limit their access to you from nine to five on week days only, and the gardener will have to stop smoking while mowing the lawn because you don't want your kids having to inhale smoke at the swing set.

 Expansion means things are going to change, and that can be scary.

When you stop pushing down your feelings with addictive behaviors, and give yourself the space to expand into the more powerful and vibrant version of yourself, the world around you is going to go through growing pains too. That's the risk we take in order to grow and live into the truth of who we are. In the words of Anais Nin, "And the day came when the risk to remain tight in a bud was more painful than the risk it took to blossom."

We are constantly challenged to sustain the expansion we've achieved. It's not uncommon for us to struggle at the mercy of self-sabotaging behavior. Shadow, the dark, repressed, unresolved, avoided "stuff" that is wreaking havoc in your life, precisely because you're masterfully managing to convince yourself that it doesn't exist, is what discourages your expansion through the energy leaking affects of self-sabotage.

Connie Zwieg and Steven Wolf write of this shadow in their book, *Romancing the Shadow,* "[But] unconsciously, the shadow knows its purpose: It seeks to make the unconscious conscious; it tries to tell its secret. Through repeated patterns of addictive or abusive behavior . . ."

So the energy discharging behavior of addiction is actually the shadow's attempt to get your attention, "Hey you, wake up, there's something for you to look at and heal," in other words!

In Connie and Steven's words, "Shadow-work enables us to alter our self-sabotaging behavior so that we can achieve a more self-directed life. It expands our awareness to include a wider range of who we are so that we can attain more complete self-knowledge and eventually feel more genuine self-acceptance." If that's not a great definition for expansiveness, I don't know what is!

I highly recommend *Romancing the Shadow* and all books by Debbie Ford for exploring more about shadow and how to dance with it in an effective and life transforming way.

In the Vividly Woman Embodied Leader Training, we dance with shadow to make peace with what scares us and empower ourselves to live in our truth instead of our story. Shamanic rituals and soul dance journeys facilitate our exploration and safe encounter with the experiences from the past that have lodged in our body and psyche and are messing with our ability to sustain expanded states of energy.

One very powerful example from my life happened when I was participating in a ropes course with a small group. I never knew how terrified I was of heights and ropes until that day. We were asked to find a partner who would be with us for the entire ropes activity, made up of four stations, each one a different ropes adventure.

I felt happy when, Steve, a friendly fellow from Seattle, motioned toward me and we were paired. Then as a group we made our way to the first station. There it was, a six-foot-wide ladder with rungs each about four feet apart suspended up in the air demanding that I be harnessed and climb twenty-five feet up a pole in order to get to that first rung. I'd never been in a harness before. To say that I was uncomfortable with what was about to happen is putting it mildly. The activity facilitator asked, "Which pair would like to go first?" Steve shot up his hand, "We will!" he said. Well the moment he said that I went into utter shock and emotional breakdown.

As we approached the pole to get harnessed, the tears started welling in my eyes; I practically went numb as the harness began making its way onto my body. Then Steve said to me, "Okay, Leela, so here's the plan, you'll go up first, and I'll help you from behind, and we'll maneuver all the way to the top rung. We can do it." At that point everything I'd been holding back burst out in an emotional torrent. I was absolutely terrified. My whole body was shaking; I couldn't even get words out to respond.

Fortunately, Steve, bless his heart, had the wisdom to come over to me and gently say, "Don't worry, Leela, we'll only go as high as you feel comfortable, it will be great however far we get." That did calm me down a tad.

Checking in with my body, what I understood was that moving beyond this fear would take me out of the little girl role I'd played my whole life. This was a comfortable role. I'm the baby amongst my siblings. I have no biological children, and I've accommodated the need for others in my life to play the grown up while I play the helpless one. Shedding that role would inevitably mean shaking up my intimate and closest relationships, especially with my siblings and my mother. It wasn't the physical risk that was most scary in other words; it was the risk of losing my relationships that had found a comfortable status quo existence. Would I still be loved and taken care of if I expanded beyond my identity as the baby, the helpless one, the flower child archetype that my mother often referred to me as?

Having to make a conscious choice to expand beyond that role was like grieving the loss of those I held most dear. Did I consciously know that's what I'd been living, embodying the helpless baby who couldn't support herself, never made enough money, was always running up debt, and often had to rely on my partner to foot the bill? No, the baby role was a shadow character that was living inside me, and was now being invited to be released to make room for a more responsible, mature woman.

Coming into conscious awareness of this was the blessing of that experience. It didn't even matter whether I climbed up or stayed on the ground anymore. What mattered was that I take some steps in the direction of living into a more mature version of myself, trusting that the love I cherished from my family would be intact, and if it wasn't it would be necessary to let it go in favor of my love for myself and my personal expansion.

I took that step by doing my best in the ropes course and finding out that as I expand, I am still loved by my family who actually do want the best for me. And, amazingly, over time my money issues stopped perpetuating themselves. I didn't need them anymore to win me love.

All the nervous emotional release was my energetic body feeling like it couldn't tolerate the expansion because of the risk of the love I would lose. I chose to ground my energy and risk the containment, to find out that I came out more alive and more the authentic powerful me!

This story illustrates not only the issue of shadow but also the dance of boundaries in our relationships. We started exploring boundaries in an earlier chapter and we'll expand on it within the context of Harness.

Harnessing in Relationships

In relationship, boundaries are essential. The more I contain my energy, the more you can trust that I am being true to myself and more authentically present for our union. Different relationships and circumstances elicit different boundaries. Often a certain relationship or situation has a characteristic boundary that we automatically step into out of habit. Awareness helps us to make necessary choices rather than be run by unconscious patterns or external factors, and facilitates a depth of meaning in relation to our own felt Sense of boundaries.

Boundaries are a natural and essential part of relationships. Our ability to notice our boundaries when we relate will help us to stay in our power, remain in our integrity, and encourage authenticity and true intimacy, harnessing our own power for the expanded power of the relationship. To explore our sense of boundaries it's helpful to reflect on relationships that challenged us in the past. One of my early work relationships exemplifies this well.

As a bodyworker, coach, and yoga teacher I've had the pleasure of working at holistic health centers where warmth and devotion to open hearted communication were valued. Working for Jake at his healing retreat was different. His expression of anger, dissatisfaction, and judgment were common every day occurrences. His anger brought up for me the anger I had experienced with other important men in my life. His critical nature tended to feed the judgments I held about myself and reminded me of the anger I can easily turn inward.

When I began to practice taking a deep breath and drawing an imaginary boundary around my body during our interactions, I magically started to sense my own power when in his presence. I could let him be who he is and how he is and I no longer took on his negative projections. My boundary acted like a bubble distinguishing me from him and his issues that were truly not mine. I expanded my sense of self by harnessing my energy through the use of my boundary, and in so doing I used my body energy to teach Jake how to treat me.

Honoring your authentic felt sense boundaries is essential for personal expansion, but it isn't always the easiest road. There can be many hurdles to leap over before the dust settles. This was my experience with the tumultuous ending of my first marriage to Edward.

After everything we'd gone through around my infertility and the adoption falling through, was it any surprise I was feeling a little insecure? So insecure, in fact, that I was uncomfortable with a friendship he was cultivating with Joanne, a woman in our community. I had a fixed boundary regarding their involvement. Simply put, I was jealous. I didn't want him spending time with her because I could sense they were growing closer than just friends. He said she was too good a friend for him to give her up for our marriage, and sure enough, as soon as I left our shared home, he began seeing her. Not only was I without my life partner, our home, and our dogs, but I then had to deal with the fact that she had them all.

Thank Goddess, time heals. I have since managed to dissolve the pain and shame I felt when yet the next hurdle arrived. About 60 days into our separation, still healing the scab of loss, Edward and I were speaking on the phone about household issues still unresolved in our moving apart. He innocently asked me, "Do you still want to have children?" I told him I'd put children on hold for the moment and that I was thinking about my career now and what I needed to do for me. Then he dropped what felt like a bomb out of the blue sky. "Joanne is pregnant."

To say I was shocked doesn't begin to describe it. What a slap in the face to my femininity! She was giving him the very thing I had longed for us to create together and on which I had rested my feminine identity—the ability to conceive, carry, and birth a child. And I couldn't give it to him because of my infertility.

It was no less than divine intervention that I'd arranged an island refuge for the winter far from the small town where we lived together. Knowing that I wouldn't have to go back home and face her growing belly and the community gossip was a saving grace in what was the most horrible moment of my life. All my deepest shame about my infertility was front and center with nowhere to hide, but I remained in my own integrity and harnessed my power. This would begin my journey of finding my femininity apart from my ability to be a mother. It would be ten years later that Vividly Woman was born, but I have no doubt that this experience was a significant seed in what became my devotion to women healing themselves and claiming their authentic feminine power.

Boundary issues can come up in any kind of relationship, however, not just romantic ones.

Healing Relationship Exercise

This exercise will help you to take a look at your boundaries in your past and present relationships. This will shed a lot of light about you and the interpersonal dynamics of those relationships.

1. Make a list of some of the most important intimate, family and work relationships you've had.
2. Review the types of boundaries we explored in Chapter 5—Sense.

   Fluid (FL): flows and changes according to the situation.

   Fixed (FX): rigid and does not easily accommodate changing circumstances.

   Contracted (C): causes one to shrink back, shut down, and/or lose power.

   Expanded (E): may cause one to be overbearing, approval seeking and/or lose a realistic sense of oneself.

   And we'll add one more for this exercise:

   Porous (P): Distinct and clear yet flexible

3. Go down your list of important relationships and rate each one according to the type of boundary you had or have within that relationship.

   This simple exercise will help you become more aware in these relationships, as well as in new ones.

Enjoy the process of getting to know yourself better by getting to know your boundary tendencies and patterns. All our relationships, especially our relationship to self, the place where all relationships begin, have so much to gain when we establish, honor, and stay curious about our boundaries.

Sexuality

The use of Harness during sexual play can be a vital tool to enhance pleasure and grow intimacy. Joan Heartfield, author of *Romancing the Beloved*, says it well when she writes, "The Beloved wants to embody itself through us."

The beloved is the spiritual life force that you and your lover have been joined together to arouse and embody to bring healing to your lives and those you touch, and at a transpersonal level, all beings on this planet.

Joan also writes, "The first level [of consciousness] is where one or both individuals think, "I want to fuck you . . . or in other words, I want to get off on you." The second level can be seen as, "I want to make love with you and I want both of us to have a good time and be satisfied." The third level can be seen as, "I want to be present with you and support the healing and awakening we both may need. Once we feel whole, I want to honor the life energy that radiates through us, and surrender to the profound awakening it offers us."

That wholeness is the ability to contain the expanded energy without needing to discharge it through ejaculation or climax. Sustaining the energy in its fullness and riding the waves of bliss and connection, are a harnessed version of sexual expression that amplify pleasure, spread it through your body, and take lovemaking from purely personal to transpersonal healing practice, often referred to as Tantra.

Light and Shadow

Harness is made up of Ground and Mobilize. It is literally taking energy in motion and grounding it (giving it a container to press up against) so that it grows. Together, Mobilize and Ground are a dance of give and take, and the more we can notice the felt experience of each in our body, the more appropriately we can apply them both so that we experience the light of Harness instead of the shadow.

The light version of Harness allows us to gently and effectively determine when and how much grounding to apply to our mobilized energy so that there's a momentum and leveraging that complements and encourages expansion. A dam with chutes that can both open and shut to varying degrees depending on the amount of water rushing toward it is a good example of a healthy light expression of a harnessing system.

Now imagine a dam where there are no chutes to open. It's likely that the force of too much water will break through or over the dam, flooding everything below it. That's too much Ground and not enough Mobilize. If on the other hand you open too many chutes you may loose the energetic force and bring the power to a trickle. Spending your capital so that your interest all but disappears is another example of this dynamic. These are both examples of the shadow expression of Harness.

As we move into our next texture, Express you'll see how Express and Harness also dance together to create a sublime and sweet experience of effortlessness and ease. My favorite sensual example is when you're riding a bike, and you get up to the highest gear, your speed has built momentum, and now the resistance (Grounding) is actually feeding the power of your pedaling (Mobilizing) so that it feels effortless. You flow into an altered state that's a beautiful experience of Express because you were able to first Harness. This is precisely the beauty and magic of Harness; a self-replenishing and self-sustaining system that allows us, in an embodied way to work easier, live more joyfully, attract more at a vibrational level and live congruently with less suffering and heartache.

Emotional Power

Within the Vividly Woman Solar System, Harness is a planet that constellates around the sun center, mainly around the Emotional Power dimension of the sun center. Harness corresponds to our Emotional Power because it is made up of both Mobilize, which is all about heart meaning, and Ground, which is in service to expand that. So while there is certainly the Sensual Power aspect of Harness that comes with Ground, it's predominantly resonant with Emotional Power and wisdom.

The Dance of the Masculine and the Feminine

The masculine brings with it essential qualities that are necessary for the beauty in our world. The masculine offers the banks of the flowing river so that it flows instead of floods, the outer casing of the tree we call the trunk bark that allows the sap direction and encasement to grow branches skyward so we are provided oxygen, and the masculine penetrating quality of the sun is what encourages our food to grow to sustain us.

Just as the masculine and feminine exist in nature, they exist within us and finding the ways that the masculine best serves our inner feminine is the wisest and most effective way to dance with it within us and around us.

Recently in a Vividly Woman monthly Community Tele-circle we gathered to reflect and share about the dance of the masculine and feminine in our lives. It's clear that there is a preoccupation now for women to nourish more of our feminine nature to make up for the over abundance of masculine energy we've been inundated with. But is this all that's needed? Don't we also need to identify the ways that the masculine supports and nourishes the feminine, and enroll those aspects of ourselves to expand our inner feminine aliveness?

 The masculine can be wisely harnessed to leverage the feminine.

Here are some qualities of both:

Masculine qualities

> Boundaries
> Direction
> Force
> Commitment

Feminine qualities

> Fluidity
> Spontaneity
> Ease
> Devotion

Let's look at how we can pair up these qualities to optimize, enhance, and grow our selves, our vision, and our planet, using the qualities of the masculine to harness and expand the qualities of the feminine.

The freedom loving aspect of our fluid feminine nature, that loves to daydream and absorb us in the moment through our senses, could be harnessed and bounded by the masculine to amplify our rich sensuality and make it even more potent.

The spontaneity of our creative feminine wildness could benefit from some sense of masculine direction to harness the power of that wildness, apply it to a desired goal and achieve it.

The masculine force of a motor facilitates a feminine ease of travel.

And the masculine quality of commitment becomes necessary when all the feminine essence devotion in the world just isn't enough to sit through the football season with your husband in exchange for him attending the flower show with you last spring.

The fact that we have been so immersed in the masculine energetic for so long qualifies us as experts, unfortunately often to the exclusion of our feminine blessings. Perhaps the answer is not to throw out the baby with the bath water so to speak, but to creatively and wisely interweave the gifts of the masculine to support and expand the blessings of the feminine.

Look around at your life and see where you're using mostly masculine or mostly feminine qualities. Then determine if a dash of the opposite could be useful there. Instead of thinking "How can I balance one with the other?" think, "How can I enhance, grow, or optimize one with the other?"

The dance of the masculine and the feminine is indeed a dance where each has a chance to lead, follow, and be informed by the other in a constant feedback dynamic. It's how this planet continues to exist and flourish, and how we can too!

Harness Goddess

I have chosen Gaia as the Goddess of Harness. She is personified as the Great Mother and Earth herself because of her life giving and sustaining qualities.

Harness Icon

A well-known and revered woman who captures the energy of Harness is Oprah Winfrey. With multiple vehicles for self-expression; television, film, publication, and philanthropy, Oprah has grounded her passion in a meaningful productive way as to largely become our reference for success, not only for herself but for all those she endorses as well.

Other Harnessers offered by Vividly Woman Sisters are J.K. Rowling, Amelia Earhart, and Marie Curie.

Harness at Work

Harness is an essential aspect of business. In fact, I believe that business success is entirely dependent on it. You cannot hope to have a business grow without it. Harness, when applied to business is all about working more efficiently to achieve bigger and better results with less effort. Less effort and more revenue is the name of the game in business, and this is exactly what Harness enables.

I went through a harnessing growth phase in the business of Vividly Woman when my apprentices graduated to the level of facilitators. With their new status they were now able to hold the space for live events entirely on their own. This meant that I could stay home while they travel, and that we could also have multiple events going on at once, leveraging time, resources, and generating more income. This is the essence of Harness.

Developing systems, policies, and protocols, documenting all the business practices that allow your business to function, streamlining operations, these are all harnessing strategies. In my own business, this has been a fantastic process of getting more conscious and more efficient. The process of organizing so that others can look after things, has given me the opportunity to review operations with a fine tooth comb and make adjustments and modifications. This process of refining as you document is in itself a part of making a business a better-oiled machine for optimal performance.

Harness in Relationship to the Textures

The keyword for Harness in relationship to the other textures is *sustain*. Our choice to ground in meaningful action cultivates a sustained power that Harness inspires, encouraging a sense of home within.

Chapter 8 Summary: Harness

~ The Vividly Woman texture of Harness is the act of containing (grounding) energy in motion (mobilized energy) in order to expand it. When we enclose or block energy it naturally grows its force and power.

~ Harnessing emotions is empowering, while suppressing emotions is disempowering.

~ Harnessing energy is a mature and wise use of your resources

~ Addiction is literally the subconscious attempt to leak the energy that harnessing has managed to accumulate.

~ Our ability to notice our boundaries when we relate to others will help us to stay in our power and remain in our integrity, encouraging authenticity and true intimacy; harnessing our own power for the expanded power of the relationship.

~ All our relationships, especially our relationship to Self, the place where all relationships begin, have much to gain when we establish, honor and stay curious about our boundaries.

~ Harnessed sexual energy is the ability to contain the expanded energy without needing to discharge it through ejaculation or climax.

~ Shadow issues are what discourage your expansion through the energy-leaking effects of self-sabotage.

~ Harness, when applied to business is all about working more efficiently to achieve bigger and better results with less effort.

~ Finding ways that your inner masculine harnesses your inner feminine will support your expansion personally and professionally.

~ The keyword for Harness is *sustain*.

**To arouse your embodied power,
visit our "Harness" stimulators at**

www.VividlyWoman.com

"And the day came when the risk to remain tight in a bud was more painful than the risk it took to blossom."
~Anaïs Nin

CHAPTER 9

Express

Celebrate Truth and the Key to Intimacy

Express is the rich thick cream on the surface of the milk, the high note of Celine Dion that seems to go on forever, and the parade of colors that adorn the sky after the sun has set. It's the celebration that acknowledges the magic of the journey as well as the fruit of our labor. It's the voluptuous pumpkin that the patch was tilled and tended for.

Express is the exhilarating *whee!* on the way down after a long, hard, steep cycle up a mountain, the savasana (rest) at the end of a good yoga practice, the melting sensation of orgasm after climax.

As we learn to identify and consciously apply the first four textures, Sense, Ground, Mobilize, and Harness, we are clearing a path for juicy, fulfilling, and liberating expression. Having woven a felt Sense tapestry with each of the previous four textures, Express is the next in our energy continuum to be explored and embodied.

The more intimate the dance between Harness and Express, the more satisfying the experience of Express. Harness builds momentum; a charge that feeds upon itself. Letting small bits of the accumulated energy release (be expressed) at a time, maintains enough energy so that it keeps growing. This means that when you do eventually have the bigger release of Express, you haven't drained the tank so that you must start filling it all over again. This dance of Harness (grounded mobilized energy) and Express and the felt Sense awareness of it, are the full spectrum deliciousness of the Vividly Woman five textures!

The combination of all four previous textures is what births Express. If any one of the textures is hindered, avoided or not honored, Express will lose its richness. And though Express can look a myriad different ways, from frenzied or explosive to still and sublime, it always brings a promise of realization and fulfillment after a devoted and intentional journey to get there.

Recapitulation

Each year I spend my winters in a small waterfront village on the Pacific coast of Mexico. After months of travel facilitating circles across the US and Canada, I land in my tiny paradise, ready for rest. That's a bit of an understatement. In desperate need of stillness and simplicity is actually more accurate. And, stillness is what I weave. For almost the entire time I'm there, I never get into a motorized vehicle. I'm barefoot most of the time, and I spend as much time as possible on my Mexican blanket on the beach, practicing yoga, meditating, and breathing when I'm not dancing with the waves, the warmth, and the wind. This is truly my homecoming.

When I first arrive, over the first four days or so, I intentionally spend my days cleansing and recapitulating the months since I left Mexico about eight or nine months earlier. I reflect on every single city, adventure, circle, and bed I've slept in over that time. This is harvesting time! Acting as an insightful witness to the chapters of my life, paying attention to what has evolved, and finally bringing myself back to the present moment by way of the round trip journey of the past year. I can literally somatically sense the experience of landing in my body as I arrive back in present time at my Latin American enclave. Like the blossoming fruit, the ultimate expression of the tree's existence, this harvesting of truth and meaning is the expressive finale to each of my year cycles, allowing me to launch cleansed and clear into the New Year ahead.

This practice of recapitulation is my yearly ritual where I reflect, one at a time, on bite size portions of my life over the past nine months. Journal writing is another practice that helps me recapitulate all year long on a regular basis. Focused time of reflection of this sort, gives my mind the satisfaction of active participation in processing events so that unresolved issues are less likely to dominate my experience the rest of the time.

 Coming home is synonymous with self-love.

This recapitulation each year is also an intentional celebration of the life that I've designed. As women we need to nurture ourselves by celebrating our accomplishments, honoring our devotion, and acknowledging our journey. Yet celebrating ourselves is often something we forget to do or more likely avoid doing because of not truly loving ourselves. Self-love is a profound issue for women, and certainly interwoven into every dimension of this book. Coming home is in fact synonymous with self-love. At the Vividly Woman Embody Self Love Intensive we spend four full days excavating self-love so that we get home and love being there.

Authentic Expression

Identifying truth has been a consistent theme in this book, and is indeed a large part of the Vividly Woman Training and the essence of coming home. But identifying, and expressing truth are two different things. The courage and devotion to expressing truth are no easy path, but one that we must at least intend in order to achieve a degree of success.

When I began my forays into personal growth and spiritual awakening, what I discovered is that if I am a master of anything, it is keeping secrets, especially keeping secrets from myself. I was an expert at denying and avoiding. The freedom and permission to at last share what was being stuffed down inside me was a tremendous unburdening relief.

The very first workshop I attended was at a small retreat and training center on an Island in the Pacific Northwest. I attended the event with my therapist, Mary. Mary had attended many trainings there in the past, having completed one of her counseling certificates there through several month-long trainings. She was a "regular" on campus, a very familiar face. We were to share a room over the weekend of "Women and Body Energy." I called to make our reservations. Mary told me to mention her name, thinking we might get a better room that way.

Once we were settled in and sitting in our first circle of the weekend, Mary surprised me when it was her turn to share. She called herself arrogant and pompous for assuming that her frequency at the center would give her clout to secure a better room. She openly laughed at herself and her arrogance, purging herself of the shame she was feeling. Telling the truth, and being witnessed in the telling, allowed her to be free of the toxic shame that might otherwise have been stuffed down and infected her life. Mary's courage to share her truth in a safe place was the encouragement I needed to begin taking my own risks to share, first in the safety of circle and then to make that standard of truth more a part of my everyday life.

After getting comfortable sharing my truth in circle and with a therapist, where I knew I would be safe, my next step was to make sharing my truth a priority even when the external environment might not be so welcoming. This was the launch into creating a safe space within myself, which would ultimately be the most important place I could cultivate safety anyway. Everything you will find in this book and the Vividly Woman Training is devoted to women finding that safe place within ourselves.

 A safe space within me ripples out a safe space around me.

Each winter, my husband, Greg, comes to spend about a week each month with me at the beach. We've gotten very used to this seasonal rhythm. Both very independent, and supporting each other to pursue our truest dreams, we're comfortable taking time apart. "I'm coming to Mexico on the fifteenth," my husband joyfully announces his plan to join me in Mexico ten days after I'm due to arrive there. This means I'll have ten days to myself before he arrives. I find myself wondering if that's really enough time for me to accomplish what I'm intending, that being my period of recapitulation, cleansing, writing, and coming back to me without anyone else's needs to attend to.

Hmm . . . . "Why the fifteenth," I ask meekly, "are you getting a good price on flights on that date? Are you sure you want to come that soon, won't that mean I may not see you for a longer time because of my upcoming retreat schedule? What about our plans to go to Joshua Tree together?" The words come spewing out of my mouth in an attempt to avoid expressing the truth, which is, "I need a little more time to myself, actually." This is really scary to say. Fears that he'll feel offended, that he'll leave me, that he'll feel unloved, unwanted, rejected, and in turn will pull away and reject me paralyze me from saying what's true.

But then I get it, then I get that I am actually entitled to have my needs and plans for my retreat time and have it look the way I want and need it to look. Somehow, the switch gets flipped and I see my power to express my truth and have my preferences and plans honored and acknowledged. This awareness and the resulting action are hugely liberating for me.

So, what got in the way, when did it first happen, when and where did I learn not to tell the truth in order to manipulate other people's behavior? I don't honestly remember the offending experiences. Although there is the time I told my mother that the dessert of strawberries and sour cream she'd prepared were a disgusting combination and I was promptly spanked and sent to my room by my father. There was the time I yelled too loudly and was told to shut up and be quiet by my neighbor, and the time I was awarded the "I can swallow a volley ball award" at summer camp. All of these, and likely many more other experiences over the years, especially the early years, taught me that what I had to say and/or the way I naturally said it were not appropriate and could cause me to feel pain, so I better be very picky about what I say and how I say it, or risk feeling the pain.

But what happens when shutting down causes even more pain than the reaction to your authentic expression causes? What happens when my need to not hurt Greg so that he continues to love me becomes more important than honoring my truth and tending to my spiritual growth? Bitterness, resentment, passive aggressive behavior, etc. And with the chronic buildup of these comes the risk of depression, disease and possibly even terminal illnesses.

> ### *What Am I Not Saying Exercise*
>
> 1. Take some quiet time with your journal and write this question: What am I not saying to_____?
> 2. Fill in the blank with names of people in your life. Spend at least fifteen minutes writing freely in answer to the question above. It doesn't have to make sense or even be full sentences.
> 3. Do this exercise every day for a week.
> 4. After a week, reflect on how it feels to acknowledge what you've normally been withholding and how it feels to allow yourself space and time to express it and release the shame around it.

Expression and Shame

Shame and expression are intimate dance partners. Shame causes expression to hold itself back, limiting its appearance and freedom to realize itself. The consistent withholding of what makes us feel wrong, weak, guilty, and embarrassed brew together to create the elixir of shame. When, on the other hand we take the risk to reveal the feelings that we harbor, to be vulnerable in other words, shame gains less of a foothold, and we're no longer a prisoner of its destructive force on us.

I first identified shame as my *modus operandi*, also known as a default behavior, when I completed an emotional intelligence assessment. The counselor that interpreted my test shared with me that I scored very high on the shame scale. Suddenly, I became conscious of a habit of shame that had plagued me since at least my teen-age years. I first remember the felt Sense experience of shame shortly after my father died suddenly of a heart attack in mid-December when I was sixteen years old. Dancing at my cousin's wedding to the Village People's YMCA, in the basement of a synagogue, my father took his last breaths.

Shocked, shook up, and my life profoundly changed, I spent the Xmas holidays that year digesting the reality that my father was gone. In the New Year, after over a month of *shiva*, the traditional Jewish mourning ritual, I was encouraged to attend the sweet sixteen birthday parties of my friends. Sweet sixteens were a tradition in Montreal where I grew up. Drugs and alcohol and the party scene were already a part of my life so it was natural for me to consume these liberally. Desperately running from the pain, grief, and confusion of my recent loss, I could be seen each weekend, wasted on recreational drugs and alcohol, tearing up the dance floor, going berserk in a frenzy of expressive chaos.

Weekend after weekend of parties and dancing, I was a spectacle of whirling energy, trying desperately to not feel the pain of the recent loss. Each morning after, I'd awaken with a horrible feeling riddling my body. This was not the nausea and headache of a hangover. I intimately remember, and still sometimes experience its texture within me; a bleeding sensation in my heart that flows through all my limbs. This was my somatic embodiment of shame. Likely, I was oblivious to most of what had happened the night before, but I remembered enough to feel a penetrating, all engulfing, stream of embarrassment about my behavior, and the result was almost paralyzing. Little did I know that this would become a default experience whenever I felt I had done something wrong. Shame would become very familiar.

When I identified this habit, years later in adulthood, a lot started to make sense. I likened my shame habit to "my shame bucket." Inside this bucket lived an endless supply of black oily slime, my shame slime. Whenever something occurred to induce the feeling of shame, my habit was to stick my hand in the bucket and slime myself all over with this black slime. In hindsight I could see how for so many years I had been practically fully immersed in this slimy sludge, drowning in self-deprecation.

Each time, the shame and the slime would eventually dissolve and I was able to surface again above the self-demeaning torture. I imagine I had to deny some of the feelings in order to move beyond them, which further created shadow material, unresolved issues, adding insult to injury.

Becoming conscious of this habit was nothing short of amazing. I could now see how I was repeating the same sliming pattern over and over in my life, indulging in these periods of shaming self-abuse until amnesia or self-deceit set in so I could move on.

Identifying this habit of shame has facilitated the release of strangulation of my honest expression. Knowing how to find a safe place inside of me and in a safe and sacred circle of Vividly Woman Sisters who hold the space for my truth without comment, advice or the need to fix or change it, has helped me to shift this habit. It's not that I never revert back to this default behavior; it's just that now I notice it and can make a choice not to indulge in it. The practice that most helped me wean myself from the shame bucket was and still is *I Feel I Sense*, which I introduced in Chapter 5—Sense. It might sound something like this: When I identify the shame I've plunged into I simply say to myself, "I feel shame and I sense it in my belly. The quality of the sensation is heavy, liquid, and warm." As I name it I also intend to stay present with it instead of getting caught up in inner judgments about the event or experience that precipitated it. By staying with the sensations in my body, I affirm that it's safe for me in my body. The uncomfortable sensations soon dissolve and I'm no longer a prisoner to the pain and suffering of shame.

Releasing shame gives me more freedom to Express my truth with my partner. I know expressing my truth to be a cornerstone of our healthy intimate relationship with each other. Sharing the good, the bad, and the ugly are necessary to stay current and not let feelings build and corrode our connection. Through experience, I've seen how withholding stifles our shared joy and openness on all levels. My early years of healing helped me to learn to be vulnerable and to share the dark and not so pretty parts of me. I allowed myself to be seen, and discovered that even those parts of me could be loved and accepted. It was important to do that work and to have a loving partner who reminds me when I forget, and I still do.

 There may be more risk in revealing our light and being witnessed there.

In another stage of my spiritual awakening, I found that intimacy wasn't only about sharing the sorrowful, wounded parts of myself. I discovered that there was actually a greater risk of intimacy: to be seen in my joy. There was in fact more risk in revealing my light and being witnessed there. The freedom of orgasm holds with it a willingness to be seen in complete abandoned states of ecstasy that are similar to the openness that's required to dance freely, to sing unabashedly (even if you have what you think is a beautiful voice), or write, paint, speak publicly, etc. Sharing the celebration, as well as the pain, are paramount for authentic self-expression and the intimacy it encourages. This is why, at Vividly Woman trainings, when I witness women releasing the chains of self-judgment, fear and limitation to dance their ecstasy and be seen there, I'm touched deeply to my core.

When No Means Yes

One of the best things that we as women can learn how to do is to identify when our *no* actually is our *yes*. Saying no is, for a lot of us, really hard to do. For all kinds of reasons, which mostly all amount to risking losing love, no is a bit of hurdle to get over, embrace and make a frequently used word in our vocabulary.

I learned a beautiful practice for finding and saying my authentic no called the *Sacred Spot Initiation*. I first had the blessing to experience it with Caroline Muir and Joan Heartfield at their Divine Feminine Initiation weekend. I was so moved by this initiation that we now facilitate it as part of the Vividly Woman Embodied Leader Training.

The sacred spot is possibly more familiar to you as the G-spot. "Discovered" by a German gynecologist Ernst Graffenburg, the sacred spot is located within a woman's vagina and is known to both potentiate enormous physical and emotional pleasure for a woman and, unfortunately, store profound shame, pain, and trauma. Made up of spongeous tissue, it absorbs past abuse related to a woman's sexuality and becomes numb to its potential for pleasure. The sacred spot is only one portion of the vagina that has a great capacity for experiencing pleasure. (We actually prefer to call the vagina the Sanskrit or yogic term, "yoni," which acknowledges her as a sacred versus merely an anatomical part of us.) The sacred spot's trauma absorbing tendency, however, and its ability to induce female ejaculation make it unique.

In the Sacred Spot Initiation, women create and hold a safe and nurturing space for each other and massage each other's sacred spot. On a physical level, this can help release some of the stored pain and shame that live there. On an emotional level, it rewires us to know that we can choose when, how, and by whom we want to be touched. On a spiritual transpersonal level, we offer this healing of our own body and soul, for the healing of all women and our right to choose in each moment what is right and true for us. We'll explore transpersonal healing more in Chapter 14—Spiritual Lens.

Talk about a body-consciousness raising practice! It's profoundly awakening to have the choice, moment-by-moment, step-by-step, as to how, how much, and when the giver of the healing session touches me. In how much of my life and my lovemaking do I let myself be maneuvered according to someone else's needs? How many times have I repeated this scenario over and over during my lifetime, ingraining within my heart, my mind, and my tissues that I do not have the right to choose for myself.

When I model this practice during the VW Trainings, I teach women that staying present and deciding what is true in each moment; learning how to say *no* as a *yes* to *me*, is transformational, richly empowering, and an essential habit to develop for finding your way home. In the words of songstress Karen Drucker, "When I say No to you I set myself free."

Light and Shadow

Express can be a many faceted diamond that reflects beauty and clarity, or it can be used as a weapon that inflicts pain.

The shadow side of Express is overt, exaggerated, irresponsible elocution whether verbal or non-verbal. Crashing other people's boundaries, demanding others be a witness to your expression, blaming and abusing others are all an abusive use of Express that is its dark side.

"You never respected your father, you ignored him and treated him badly," these words were lashed out at me by mother days after my father had a massive heart attack and died. Uttered at a time when my mother was obviously in shock and tremendously distraught, little did she know that these words would have resounding repercussions on the rest of my life.

Expression has the power to direct our course. Being too careful about our expression is controlled and contrived; being too liberal with expression can be irresponsible, inappropriate, and damaging.

The light aspect of Express is a harnessed sensibility that allows us to know how much, why, and with whom is our self-expression appropriate. Knowing that we have no right to assume others should be a witness to our expression, and having the maturity to be able to harness our thoughts without needing to diffuse the energy they might be harboring, are all light versions of this texture.

The expressive arts are a powerful modality for therapeutic healing that Harnesses the light aspect of Express. Dance, painting, story telling or any other creative medium takes us on a journey to discover more about ourselves. The premise is that lodged in the psyche are subconscious truths that can be assisted to become conscious, and therefore be healed, though artistic expression.

We touched on this in Chapter 4—Emotional Power, where we looked at how it's essential to express and cleanse ourselves of toxic emotional buildup on a regular basis so that we don't make ourselves sick. The use of creative modalities can assist in this process.

Anna Halprin was a pioneer of the Expressive Arts Therapy movement, helping cancer victims to discover and heal the psycho-spiritual manifestation of their disease. After healing her own cancer, Halprin founded the Tamalpa Expressive Arts Institute in California where I had the privilege of studying.

Waiting vs. Procrastination

Expression doesn't necessarily imply action. It can actually appear as stillness to the outside world. Always taking action may seem like the most effective thing to do in order to get things done and off your plate. But there is a time and a place where just waiting, no action yet, is the wisest thing and what your intuition is telling you.

In Intuitive Power we distinguish between intuition and ego, and we see that making a decision between options based on whether they're in alignment with ego or intuition is a helpful way to get clear and make healthy choices. However, what if neither option is a fit? What if there's a third option, and that option is to wait? Distinguishing between waiting and procrastination and how they each express themselves in your life and in your body is a valuable tool to have.

"In the past I have viewed waiting as procrastination. This has always been a huge struggle for me. Since my only method of decision-making was via my head/mind, I naturally made choices whether I was ready to or not. I was in Mobilize mode all the time regardless of the foolish and impulsive choices I made. I had no way of determining how to act but I was great at reacting . . . I didn't understand the difference," wrote Helena in her Coach Training homework.

In Express, we have the added wisdom of Harness that tempers our Mobilize so that instead of seeing stillness as procrastination, we recognize waiting as a mature and informed expression of energy management.

Waiting vs. Procrastination Exercise

1. Identify a decision that you've needed to make but have been struggling with so that it has gone undecided for what seems like a long time.

2. Identify the two options that you are torn between. *Body Source* to determine which is more ego and which is more intuition. Review Chapter 4—Intuitive Power if you need help.
3. Add a third option: Wait for events to unfold to get clear about my direction.
4. Ask yourself this question: "When I give myself the option of waiting, is that different than what I think of as procrastination?"
5. *Body Source* waiting. *Body Source* procrastination.
6. Make note of what you identified from the process above.

Express Goddess

Hawaiian Goddess Pele is known as the Goddess of Fire, Lightning, Wind, and Volcanoes. Pele is also celebrated for her creative power, passion, purpose, and profound love. An ally to those who desire to transcend the illusions of fear and limitation, she is devoted to helping us realize and express our creative power in a way that brings benefit, blessings, and beauty to the whole.

Pele was harassed and shunned by jealous snow goddesses and by her own sister who tried to extinguish Pele's fire at every chance she had, using tidal waves and unrelenting water to force Pele to leave whenever she attempted to settle somewhere. Pele persevered and eventually found her home on the Big Island of Hawaii in the volcano called Kilauea (which means spreading).

Pele's devotion to her inner flame reminds us that when we know and honor who we are, valuing our own true self we will find our right place (home). She also invokes the persistence to persevere despite perceived obstacles when we are pursuing our true path. We're inspired to not give up just before we reach the destination of our dreams.

Her forms are many, including the volcano, lava, and fire/flame. Goddess Pele also has the ability to shape-shift and will show herself as a beautiful young woman or as a Crone.

Icon

One of the *"*shero*es"* of our time who captures the essence of the Express archetype is Erin Brockovitch. Driven to take and maintain a stand for what she believed in, Brockovitch would stop at nothing to see justice served in her fight for clean water. She's become a legend and an icon of human integrity and passionate expression.

We added Jane Fonda, Lady Gaga, and Mae West to the Express icon list for each expressing her truth in her own authentically unique way.

Express at Work

If you're devoted to any kind of success through your job or business one fantastic way to start attracting that success to you is by celebrating all the little wins and achievements along the way. Express teaches us that the journey isn't complete until we've acknowledged our efforts and all the ways we've applied our passion. If we want our clients, the public, and the world at large to take note of our talents and services and become consumers of them, we need to make a regular practice of appreciating what we offer ourselves through spontaneous, as well, as planned acts of celebration.

Express in Relationship to the Textures

The keyword for Express is *celebration*. Express is the icing on the cake that celebrates the journey through each of the other four textures. Celebrating the *way home* and the *being home* are both aspects of Express.

Chapter 9 Summary: Express

~ The dance of Harness (grounded mobilized energy) and Express with the felt Sense awareness of that dance, are the full spectrum power of The Vividly Woman five textures.

~ Recapitulation is an act of celebrating my life that gives my mind the satisfaction of active participation in processing events so that unresolved issues are less likely to dominate my experience the rest of the time.

~ The most important place to cultivate safety is within ourselves.

~ When we take the risk to reveal what makes us feel wrong, weak, guilty, and embarrassed we are no longer a prisoner of shame's destructive force on us.

~ Avoiding authentic expression in order to manipulate the behavior of others will lead to bitterness, resentment, and passive aggressive behavior that can cause disease, illness, and even death.

~ Saying *no* to another, as a *yes* to me is an empowering and essential practice of women's embodied leadership.

~ Intimacy is not only about sharing our sorrowful, wounded parts. It can actually be a greater risk of intimacy to share the truth of our joy. Sharing the celebration, as well as the pain, are important for authentic self-expression and the intimacy it encourages.

~ There is a time and a place where just waiting, no action, is the wisest thing and what your intuition is telling you. Waiting is not always procrastinating.

~ The keyword for Express is *celebration*.

**To arouse your embodied power,
visit our "Express" stimulators at**

www.VividlyWoman.com

LENSES

Portals to Wisdom

The Vividly Woman Solar System

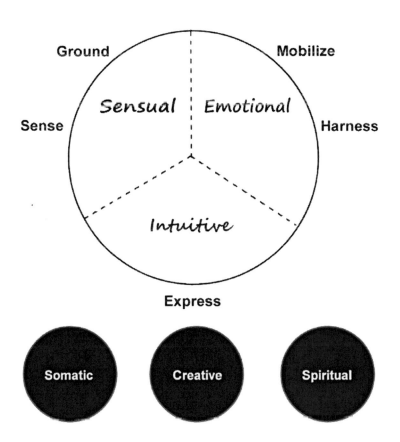

CHAPTER 10

Lenses

How We Look Determines What We See

"See a world in a grain of sand and eternity in an hour." William Blake

Together we've dived into reclaiming the inner wisdom of our power centers and charting the path of the textures toward a more mature relationship to energy. Our next stop on the journey to embodied power takes us to the lenses. Used as tools of self-inquiry, the lenses help us to discover more about ourselves and leverage our understanding and embodiment of the centers and textures.

A lens is defined as a molded piece of glass, plastic, or other transparent material used to form an image for viewing. How we see the things before us depends entirely on the lens we choose to look at them through. Each of my eyes sees things radically differently, so much so that my prescription glasses would have me walking in circles if I swapped the lenses from side to side.

A camera is characterized by the type and depth of lens it uses, and the photographs it produces are a product of its lens. As Wayne Dyer says, "When you change the way you look at things, the things you look at change."

In the Vividly Woman world of embodied power, we understand that insight is influenced by our point of access, and that we have the right to choose our point of access at all times.

The Vividly Woman lenses are all about that choice. We have the power to choose how we perceive and experience the world around us and in relationship to us. Each of the three Vividly Woman lenses gives us a unique and valuable insight into our situation or issue. By exercising our right to choose how we look at and inquire into circumstances, we make a powerful statement about our devotion to raising our consciousness, our emotional maturity, and our self-responsibility.

Kim, for example, grew up in a Mennonite community. She was taught that the body was bad and shameful. Sexuality, dance, and femininity were shunned and encouraged to stay hidden. As a result, Kim grew up believing that it wasn't safe to be feminine. Her mother downplayed her femininity, and as is common in households within sexually repressed societies, there may even have been sexual abuse or incest, even if it was on a very subtle, covert level.

Kim married and had two sons. She went from being a child in an environment void of feminine sensuality and beauty into motherhood, caring for her sons and her husband in a testosterone-rampant setting that perpetuated the seeds of repression planted in her upbringing.

Spending time in sacred circle, and practicing rituals that reconnected her to the feminine beauty inherent in nature, Kim came to see that she could choose how to look at the world. She discovered it was safe to see through the eyes of her womanhood, and interface with the world from her sensual, spiritual, and creative aliveness, all the things that she'd been shutting down because they were too feminine, not safe. Witnessing Kim's homecoming to her power of choice has been one of the most beautiful awakenings I've had the gift of experiencing.

The Vividly Woman lenses help us unlock doors and ignite the flame of feminine richness that we've spent so much time ignoring in favor of a more linear and masculine way of being in the world and working through challenges and obstacles. The lenses are a feminine approach that doesn't so much intend to solve problems, as to intend to create space for us to discover the gifts, blessings and lessons inherent in every circumstance. This more lateral, feminine focused perspective adds depth and meaning to the journey that is our life.

Each of the three Vividly Woman lenses: Somatic, Spiritual, and Creative sets us off on an odyssey of harvesting awareness that aids us on our quest for greater peace, fulfillment, and self-realization. Although each lens is a jumping off point that will inspire a multitude of explorative questions and queries, each lens has one main question:

Somatic Lens: Where does this issue live in your body and what are the sensations there?

Creative Lens: What is the creative opportunity here?

Spiritual Lens: How am I being used?

Vividly Woman Coaches are trained to midwife you through any life situation or challenging issue using the lenses and associated questions and prompts, to be mirrors and sounding boards as they peer with you through the lenses at whatever is current and up for you.

But the beauty of the lenses is that they are portals into your wisdom and power that you can employ on your own. Regardless of what's stirring within you or around you, the lenses are a juicy and empowering way to find your way home.

In Chapters 11-13 we'll explore how each of the lenses might already be showing up in your life, how to harness their power, and how to become more masterful at using every life situation as a launching pad for personal embodied power.

Chapter 10 Summary: Lenses

~ Insight is influenced by our point of access and we have the right to choose our point of access at all times.

~ The lenses are a feminine approach that doesn't so much intend to solve problems, as much it intends to create space for us to discover the gifts, blessings, and lessons inherent in every circumstance.

~ Every life situation is a launching pad for personal embodied power.

"The female soul resides in the guts, not in the head".
~ Clarissa Pinkola Estes

CHAPTER 11

Somatic Lens

Resource Your Body's Truth

The Somatic Lens is everything body, everything physical, everything of the soma!

The Somatic Lens is the first stop on our lens adventure. It corresponds to and awakens our Sensual Power in that it guides us to become intimately aware of what is alive within our body temple. With this skill in our quiver of embodiment tools, we have enhanced access to our Emotional and Intuitive Power as well.

If you've been on a spiritual path, devoting yourself to your higher consciousness and expanding spiritual awareness, you may have been ignoring or not prioritizing and resourcing your body for spiritual awakening.

This is an unfortunate reality that's all too common, especially in the world of religion that's dominated by a masculine perspective. As the feminine gains her rightful status, we're now seeing a shift. The prevalence of yoga in mainstream and sexuality moving more into the domain of the sacred are evidence of our cultural and collective awakening and rising consciousness. We certainly still have a long way to go but there have been huge steps in the right direction.

The Somatic Lens takes you into the realm of your body's wisdom, intelligence, and truth. It asks you to ask your body for the insights and intuition that are embedded and stirring within your tissues, and heed that information, and to actually celebrate it. It's fascinating to me that most people on this planet of ours walk around having body experiences, constant body sensations, and physical feedback; yet, they are completely numb and shut off from those cues and messages. It's like having a GPS on in your car, but you keep going in the completely opposite direction or ignoring the commands and instructions. We've become so deadened to the GPS that we don't even hear it anymore and take its voice for granted like incessant and unimportant background music.

One of the main reasons we get sick, develop terminal illnesses, and feel helpless about our physical health is this chronic ignoring of the body's truth. We just don't know how to listen to the wise woman voice that's nagging within to wake up and smell the coffee. The tendency to refer outside of ourselves for answers, whether to the doctor, the mirror, or the media is a disempowering default that we have to unlearn in order to live in our embodied power.

The *Somatic Lens Practice* is a way of peering inside with curiosity and fascination for the subtle palette of sensations that lives and dances within. Every moment of every day your body is having an experience, and that experience is being communicated to you in temperature, texture, quality, and a myriad of other possible distinctions. To listen to these and to heed their message is to harness and acknowledge that we may be spiritual beings but we are most certainly living in a physical body. This physical body is actually quite brilliant at self-preservation, and can tell you about its current state in every moment. It starts off with a whisper and creeps into a louder expression when you don't listen, eventually erupting into disease when it's ignored long enough.

When there's something troubling afoot your body reacts in its own special way depending on what's up. Whether you're happy, sad, excited, bored, or indifferent, your body always has something to say about it. Unfortunately, our minds, influenced by past experience, and often the need to be loved and accepted by others, get in the way of hearing the pristine truth being spoken by the body. Intentionally cultivating a listening awareness to the body's experience can tell us lots about what's *really* going on.

Janice, for example, began a coaching session by telling me that she'd recently lost her biggest client. Most of her business stemmed from this client, and though she had sought to expand her client list for several years, she was never able to significantly add other major ones. Fortunately, the gravy train kept delivering, and she decided to sit back and enjoy the ride instead of constantly worrying about changing anything.

She came to the session feeling worried and shocked, with all kinds of negative thoughts brewing within her. Self-blame, anger, and confusion were all up for her.

"What's happening in your body? Where do these feelings live?" I asked her, applying the Somatic Lens.

"Well, I can sense the worry in the top of my chest. It's like a heaviness resting like a dead wait there. The shock is like numbness in my head. I can feel sadness, and I sense that in my belly."

"Great awareness," I said. "Now can you just sit with all of that? Can you give those feelings and the corresponding sensations, and any others that arise within you, the space and the time to just simmer, without having to go up in to your head to explain or justify them?"

"Yes," she said.

We sat for a few moments while she gave herself permission to have the feelings and sensations.

"What's happening now?" I asked.

"I just feel this profound experience of peace. The feelings aren't tugging at me like before and I feel an experience of self-love and tenderness that wasn't there before. It seems to be saying it's okay to have these feelings."

"Beautiful," I said. "It sounds like your body was really wanting your attention and you've honored its need to be heard and sensed."

The dialogue above is typical of a Vividly Woman Coaching Session, especially when there's something really triggered for a client. It's a great example of how the Somatic Lens works to establish a neutral place to examine a life situation. We call this practice of asking our body for information *Body Sourcing*. In the next chapter we'll see how Janice used the Creative Lens to discover more about herself in relation to this issue.

In one of our Coach Training calls on teaching how to use the Somatic Lens, I shared how I had identified the felt Sense experience of blame in my body when my husband had disappointed me the previous weekend. Instead of getting carried away with the story of blame and why he was wrong, dumping it on him, and letting it further spread toxins through my body, I chose to acknowledge the sensation of blame in my body, give it space, and allow it to dissolve.

Lori shared this in response to my sharing "Oh, how often do I get into that story and hurt myself. You're so right; no matter what the story is it has to end with me because I perpetuate my suffering needlessly and endlessly! Thank god for *Body Sourcing* . . . my salvation."

When we are in the grip of the emotions, struggling to make sense of them with our head, the body is fighting to have its experience acknowledged. Ignoring the body and focusing on the mind's story just makes it all more traumatic. The Somatic Lens helps us to ground and calm, to dissolve the reactions, and cleanse ourselves of the unhealthy self-blame patterns or story telling victim routine.

 There are as many past as present issues being triggered when we find ourselves having strong feelings and reactions.

The Somatic Lens lets us disconnect from the story entirely. Instead of needing to justify what's stirring within, we give it permission to just be, and allow the energy of the situation to breathe. The reality is that though there may be a current issue that is triggering all the feelings, there are as many past issues, and their associated feelings, that are being triggered simultaneously. These need to be allowed to resurface instead of getting instantly squelched by rational thoughts and explanations. That only serves to suffocate the feelings, and like when you squeeze a balloon, the air (feelings) will just pop up somewhere else causing chaos in your life when least expected. All the more reason to let our feelings have their space and flow through without attaching too much meaning.

Somatic Lens Self Practice

If you can remember to take a couple of moments whenever uncomfortable feelings surface to ask yourself, "Where does this live in my body, what are the sensations, and what is my body asking to have attention paid to?" you will effectively be using the Somatic Lens.

Besides avoiding further self-betrayal and stuffing of feelings, you are also giving your psyche a powerful message: "My body matters, she knows the truth and I'm choosing to listen to her." When you get into the habit of this practice, you'll be making an important shift in your consciousness toward a more embodied aliveness. Imagine months and years of this kind of behavior and how it would alter your current relationship with your body from just something that you drag around with you, to a vital and wise dimension of your being that you love, respect, and resource.

Tracking Sensation

Sensation is the language of your body. Tracking body sensation is a habit of bringing your awareness to your body sensations. It is a skill that comes with practice.

Tracking sensation is an excellent way to bring yourself into the present, get out of your head, ground into your body and notice the way energy moves within you. It is an effective way to live a more sensual, vivid existence.

At first tracking sensation can be elusive, like mercury. What is a sensation? How do I know if that's really happening or if I'm making it up? These are questions that the mind may throw at you to distract you from staying in your body. By allowing the questions to be there, without needing to answer them, you remind yourself to stay with your body.

On the continuum from numb to hypersensitive there are an infinite number of points on this journey of sensation and body awakening. Staying present and fascinated by the dance of energy within will take you on an adventure into a rhapsodic universe of sensations made up of temperature and textures that may range from neutral, comfortable, pleasurable, to painful. Curiosity, equanimity, and acceptance will encourage your ability to make this a habit and practice that serves you.

Tracking Sensation Practice

You'll need a comfortable place to lie down and be undisturbed for at least ten minutes, a music source, and an instrumental piece of music that you've chosen and are ready to play.

1. Create your comfortable place for practice
2. Set up your music so it's ready to play
3. Read the guided meditation below, following the directions or download the audio version to listen to the "Somatic Lens" stimulator at www.VividlyWoman.com
4. Begin music
5. Lie down and watch the music dance through you as you track the corresponding sensations.

Tracking Sensation Guided Meditation

Take a nice deep breath in through your nose, fill your belly and then let the breath out with a sigh. Notice what sensations are present for you. An itch, part of your body against the floor, temperature sensations, a breeze across your cheek, an ache, etc.

Breathe and notice.

(Pause reading for a few breaths to allow time for tracking sensation, including the sensation of the breath dancing in and through you).

When you get into the habit of identifying sensations you will start to notice that sensations arise as feelings do within you.

> You can learn to identify feelings through the sensations they create and thereby be more present, authentic, and more routinely tend to those feelings rather than stuff and deny them which can be a way of betraying us and encouraging disease.
>
> As you listen to the music notice sensations that arise within you, notice how different instruments speak to different parts of your body, notice how different sound qualities elicit different sensation qualities. There is an orchestra of sensation going on within you, when you stop to notice and track sensation.
>
> (Play music)

Chapter 11 Summary: Somatic Lens

- The Somatic Lens asks you to ask your body for the insights and intuition that are embedded and stirring within your tissues, and to heed that information, and actually celebrate it.
- *Body Sourcing* is the practice of asking our body for information.
- The Somatic Lens lets us disconnect from the story entirely. Without needing to justify what's stirring within, we give it permission to just be, and allow the energy of the situation to breathe.
- *Body Sourcing* moves you away from experiencing your body as just something that you drag around with you, to a vital and wise dimension of your being that you love, respect, and resource.

**To arouse your embodied power,
visit our "Somatic Lens" stimulators at**

www.VividlyWoman.com

> *"The only way I have ever understood, broken free, emerged, healed, forgiven, flourished and grown powerful is by asking the hard questions and then living into the answers through opening up to my own terror and transmuting it into creativity."*
> ~Sue Monk Kidd

CHAPTER 12

Creative Lens

Discover the Gift

Able now to resource our body's truth through the use of the Somatic Lens, we can launch into deciphering the gifts of the Creative Lens. An aspect of the Emotional Power center, the Creative Lens encourages the freedom to feel, see, and believe that anything is possible so that we can move out of the limitations of *living in the box* and into the realm of unbridled possibility.

The Creative Lens engages your heart and your imagination. It's a beautiful bridge between what you feel shouldn't be happening and the magic that these events in your life are actually birthing.

Using the Creative Lens, we discover, in the midst of uncertainty, discomfort or disappointment or all of the above, that the universe is delivering the perfect situation that will allow us one or all of the following:

1. To learn a very important self-growth lesson
2. To have a meaningful experience that would not have happened otherwise
3. To be motivated to do something that you were avoiding

The question that we use to inspire a new perspective on an otherwise obnoxious situation is "What is the creative opportunity for me here"?

While the Spiritual Lens seeks to identify the value that extends beyond your one life, the Creative Lens is all about you and your very own life dance. It chooses to see current events as a catalyst for some important missing pieces in the bigger scheme of your personal journey.

Let's look at each of the possible gifts that the Creative Lens helps us to claim.

1. Applying the Creative Lens to learn an important self-growth lesson:

Have you ever been stuck in a situation that you wish with all your heart wasn't happening? I imagine all of us have had this experience, at least a time or two. (I'm being a little facetious!) Who hasn't had let downs, unpleasant surprises or lost someone or something close to them? We all have, and when we're in the midst of it all it can be heartbreaking and wretched to have to go through the pain that comes with it. The obvious belief is "this shouldn't be happening." But if we look deeper, and identify what it is this experience is teaching us, we usually find out that it's only through life experience that we would have learned that lesson that in fact is essential for our evolution and personal expansion.

My client, Janice, in Chapter 11 sincerely wished she didn't have to lose her biggest client and suffer the fear around the loss to her business. But the reality of it happening opened her eyes to how much she was equating her own self-worth with that of her business. She acknowledged how vital it was for her to get that and to create more balance in her life, which in turn would nourish her business.

Does personal growth always require that we experience an unpleasant turn of events? No, thankfully not. But the sooner we can start suspending our judgement about whether any experience should or shouldn't be happening, in favor of a curiosity about what the gift is, the sooner we see that all life's challenges *are* actually gifts. The way we interpret events is totally up to us. The more we learn and grow, the more we're inclined to appreciate that everything happens for a reason. So the quicker you get the hang of the Creative Lens, the less you'll suffer the occurrence of what could seem like a bummer experience.

2. Applying the Creative Lens to identify a meaningful experience that would not have happened otherwise:

Events don't happen in isolation. They catalyze each other. Nothing happens unless something happened before it and, likewise, each event is a precursor to the one after it. Using the Creative Lens we can sometimes bring into conscious awareness that this seemingly unpleasant experience needed to happen in order for something else to be inspired by its occurrence. My father dying had to happen in order for me to discover dance as a healing practice for my grief. That discovery became my life's work. Do I still wish my father hadn't died when I was sixteen? Yes, but I understand that there is an opportunity for me in every eventuality, this one included.

3. Applying the Creative Lens to identify how you are motivated to do something that you were avoiding:

Unfortunate circumstances often require us to take action that wasn't planned and isn't preferred. Taking this action or actions is not your first choice and you've likely spent a lot of time avoiding it. The fact that now you have to do it is precisely why you are in the situation you are in.

Using the Creative Lens, you can identify that action and its value to you.

When my mother died a couple of days before a weeklong Vividly Woman retreat in Mexico, I felt I had no choice but to hand over the reins to my apprentices so that I could follow my truth and attend my mother's funeral in Canada and spend the week with my family. About a month earlier, a friend had asked if I was likely to step aside to give my apprentices this chance unless I was forced to. I answered that, no, I was not likely to do that. Events clearly invited me to move beyond my own willingness to a new level of trust. It was a huge step in Vividly Woman's growth as a business, allowing me as a facilitator to be duplicated, so that our program calendar could expand and we could serve more women who are craving to experience this work and its life transforming gifts firsthand.

 Humility is a vital aspect of your embodied presence.

There is a humility that can come with the application and regular practice of the Creative Lens. Being forced to accept that we aren't in control, and that maybe it's actually better that way, wakes up a sensibility and wisdom that are important steps on the journey to our embodied awakening. The sensation of letting go that can happen when humility becomes more of a theme in your life is a vital aspect of your embodied presence. It's incredibly difficult to be connected to your body when you're in a contracted and constricted state. The more we can soften, open, and create internal space, the more we can identify the vast universe of sensation that lives there and be in authentic dialogue with our body.

As the name implies, the Creative Lens requires our creative openness and happily inspires more of the same. I've heard countless times from women who feel cut off from their femininity, that they also don't feel creative. "I'm an accountant, I don't know how to be creative," is the sort of thing I've heard a lot. And, while at first glance working with numbers all day doesn't seem like a very touchy feely kind of creative thing, there is always an opportunity to shift our perspective, and this is what the Creative Lens helps us to do.

In her audio series *The Creative Fire*, Jungian psychologist, Clarissa Pinkola Estes, shares, "The creative within the soul makes the artist the artist, not the work that they produce. The creative function is the center of the soul. It can never be destroyed."

Our creativity determines how we approach what we're doing. It's not the actual activity or the outcome itself that's creative. Bringing creativity to your tasks and endeavors, whatever they may be, on a regular basis is what makes you creative. The Creative Lens is a tool that can encourage this habit and bring more color and imaginative aliveness to your daily life.

Chapter 12 Summary: Creative Lens

~ The Creative Lens engages your heart and your imagination.

~ We can choose to see current events as opportunities.

~ The quicker you get that whatever is happening is for your personal growth the less you'll suffer.

~ One experience catalyzes another. We never know what may be a stepping-stone for the next important thing that needs to happen for our life purpose to be fulfilled.

~ Using the Creative Lens helps us identify actions that we have been avoiding but which are necessary for our highest evolution.

~ Humility is an important quality to cultivate that encourages the spaciousness characteristic of embodied presence.

~ Creativity is an approach to life rather than the result of our actions.

**To arouse your embodied power,
visit our "Creative Lens" stimulators at**

www.VividlyWoman.com

"In allowing peace to prevail in our relationship with the body, in learning to live from the inside out, we offer ourselves to the Divine to be used for service".
~Christina Sell

CHAPTER 13

Spiritual Lens

Awaken Transpersonal Power

The Spiritual Lens is the perspective of the wisdom of spirit, intuition, and the transpersonal realm. Corresponding to, and a facet of, Intuitive Power, the Spiritual Lens helps you identify the dimension of your experience that's not really about you personally, but rather is about how you're being used by spirit trans-personally for healing and awakening all life.

The essence of spirit is its life infusing quality that weaves through and connects all that is alive. The wisdom to see our own existence as braided with that of all of creation gives us access to the realm of spirit. The Spiritual Lens invites us to expand beyond ego self to embody the cosmic self, in Sanskrit known as the leela, the cosmic dance or divine play of the universe. It's a consciousness that embraces our place in the rhythm of existence, transcending time and space, where all we are is energy and we can tap into and embody the true oneness that is characteristic of energy's diffuse nature.

The Spiritual Lens takes us out of our own personal story, into a bigger story.

Contrary to what religion teaches us, that we must conform our beliefs to fit an established dogma, spirituality shows us that it's our direct experience, rather than our beliefs, that matter in awakening to all that is sacred and divine. Spirituality takes us into a dimension of existence that is separate from the self or the ego. Instead of exploring how life circumstances are affecting our personality, status, goals, and aspirations, in the Spiritual Lens we look at how we as spiritual beings are merely being used for a higher evolutionary and healing purpose.

Wendy was a coaching client of mine who was grappling with the fetus growing in her womb. She had accidentally conceived with a lover whom she couldn't see herself spending a lifetime with, let alone a few years. It felt right to enroll the Spiritual Lens in our work together.

"How are you being used, Wendy? How is this pregnancy not about you, but about what you came here to do for all beings?" I asked.

"Well, I suppose, this could be about the child within me having an important mission to fulfill. I'm just here to nurture and care for him."

That's a beautiful thought," I offered, "and I wonder, in addition to what this child is bringing to our world, what is it that you, in your own life are being used for"?

Wendy was silent for a moment, and then I heard tears welling up, in her difficulty speaking.

"The love I feel for this life growing inside me is greater than any love I've ever felt, or ever could have imagined feeling. It transcends words or description. It's a profound, all pervading energy. Our world needs this kind of love. I know I can help make a difference loving in this way. I know I can even love the father, even if I don't want to create a life with him."

I could strongly relate to Wendy's awareness. Though I'd never carried a child, her experience reminded me of the tremendous love I felt and shared with my mother at the end of her life. It was the deepest intimacy I had ever known, and as painful as it was to watch her suffer and know I had to let her go, that love was so divine and so blessed, I felt like I was being used as a vessel through which to offer it to the world.

The Spiritual Lens takes us out of our own personal story, into a bigger story that's about the world, all its creatures, and existence. It asks us to consider the essence of our being-ness beyond our own little life, and reflect on how and why our presence on this planet matters. Interwoven in the tapestry of our life, interlacing the backdrop of our personal warp, the obvious pattern and narrative that the tapestry may be telling, and the weft that is the skeletal structure of our life, there are the subtle threads, the intricate weave that is the real reason we are here.

We may spend a lifetime trying to figure out what it is we're supposed to *do* with our life. What is our divine "assignment," in the words of Jungian analyst and activist Jean Shinoda Bolen, or mission that, we hope, can be expressed in our career and service. But what if, on the road to get there, all the pitfalls along the way, the setbacks, the false starts, the failures, losses, and frustrations are the true essence of our purpose here, not the home runs, the approval, and acknowledgements from the outside? The Spiritual Lens is an invitation to see the entire tapestry, not just the front side, harness it's wisdom, and live a spiritually rich life whatever the circumstances may be.

The Spiritual Lens Self Practice

The question that will support you living into your own precious life as an expression of divine order is "How am I being used?" Dare to answer this question as if your life truly matters.

In answer to this question, Deb, one of the Vividly Woman Coach Trainees shared, "I am being used for healing past, current (my family is all benefiting), and future generations. The issue I brought in for healing is abuse, which was being transferred down generation to generation. I'm being used by teaching people how to treat me, setting my boundaries, forgiving, and asking for forgiveness with the healing light shining." Practicing the use of the Spiritual Lens in her own life, Deb is acknowledging herself as a bearer of light and wisdom in the lives of others.

When in the midst of catastrophe, when it seems the most unfair, the most inconvenient and troublesome, if you can remember to ask yourself this question and be open to the answer, you'll be affirming your connection to the blessing of all life, your spiritual essence.

Chapter 13 Summary: Spiritual Lens

~ This Lens helps us affirm how we are being used by spirit transpersonally for healing and awakening all life.

~ Transpersonal awareness is a consciousness that transcends time and space, characteristic of the diffuse nature of energy.

~ Experience rather than belief is what connects us to the realm of spirit.

~ We can choose to embrace our failures as much as our successes as necessary steps on the path to our life purpose.

**To arouse your embodied power,
visit our "Spiritual Lens" stimulators at**

www.VividlyWoman.com

CHAPTER 14

Dancing the Solar System

Explore with Your Body

A conceptual understanding of the solar system has been a major motivation for this book. It was important for me to be able to illustrate the everyday living value of this system so that it can be applied and make a tangible difference in the lives of many women.

Along with the theoretical information that's now available here for you to reference, a book on embodiment would not be complete if I didn't also include the solar system's application to dance and movement so that you can deepen your embodiment of the information. At live events we use a dash of theory to complement the experiential embodiment processes. In this book we use a smattering of embodiment processes to complement the theory.

Here are some ideas for how to utilize movement to deepen your inquiry into each of the dimensions and components of the Vividly Woman Solar System. Use these as a jumping off point to dive into your version of the way home to your embodied power. Allow your insights and awarenesses to birth new ways to enrich and enliven the journey afoot.

Sensual Power

Sensual Power is located primarily in the hip, pelvic, and abdominal region. The densest of the power centers, the heavy thighbones and bulbous joint articulations at the hip's ball and socket joint offer us stability and mobility at the same time.

Common movements for range of motion freedom of the joint are hip and pelvic rotations, hip and pelvic rocking forward and back, wagging the tailbone, and shaking the booty!

Try this:

Standing on your feet with a stance that's wider than hip width, do each of the movements above. Maintain spongy, springy knees, and notice the extent of freedom in your hip joints as you do the movements. Do the same movements with your knees locked, and notice the range of motion available to you now.

Lie on your back with one leg extended and one knee bent. With the bent knee, explore space. Write your name in the air with your bent knee. Close your eyes and dive into your hips in your awareness. Notice what's occurring in your hip as you explore with your knee. Knee mobilization gives you access to greater motion in the hips.

A little known tip for how to access greater freedom in the hips is to let the jaw and the mouth relax. Try all the above movements with a relaxed jaw and slightly parted lips to notice if there's any difference. It's no surprise that kissing is such an important part of sex!

Animal Archetype:

The animal archetype for Sensual Power is the wild cat. The puma, the cougar, and tiger all hover close to the earth with spongy knees as if *milking* the earth, drawing earth energy up their hindquarters and their hips. Try this motion for yourself and notice the freedom in the hips and the arousal to your vulva area.

Music:

Music that helps us access the movement of Sensual Power are flowy syrupy sounds that elicit fluidity, succulence, and a safe gradual way of opening and warming up. Once the body opens, drumming and tribal rhythms elicit an earthy connection that accents and grounds the fluidity making the flow more viscous without sacrificing mobility.

Playlist:

> Pussycat Dolls "Feeling Good"
> Soulfood "Tantric Body"

Emotional Power

Emotional Power is located primarily in your heart, shoulders, and upper back region. The ball and socket joint at the shoulders invite yawning open of the entire back and the shoulder blades, like wings, connect the fluid arms to the torso.

Common movements here are swooping, undulating wing like arms, chest shimmy, rounding shoulders front and back, isolating the rib cage, and exploring range of motion of the scapulae or what I like to call *painting a blank canvas* with your shoulder blades.

Try this:

Explore space with your elbows. First use the pointy outside of your elbow and then the inside bend of the elbow, writing your name in the air with each of these and closing your eyes to sense inwardly, noticing the ripple into your shoulder joint and into your chest.

Animal Archetype:

The animal archetype for Emotional Power is the heron. The wide and expansive wingspan of this bird accentuates the opening and the closing of the heart that are important aspects of our wisdom and Emotional Power.

Music:

Music that helps us access Emotional Power is emotionally charged, containing sentimental lyrics, dramatic nuances or melodic patterns that tug on our heartstrings. Music has a powerful ability to connect us to our emotions. "Notes open the gateways of our hearts," writes music therapist Christine Stevens in Music Medicine.

Playlist:

>Gustav Mahler *Symphony #5 Adagietto*
>Celine Dion "My Love Will Go On"

Intuitive Power

Intuitive Power is located primarily in the region of the head and neck. This is where the sixth chakra sits, the visionary center that gives us access to higher self-wisdom.

Movements that help to open and activate this power center involve rotating the head on the shoulders, following the movement of the hands with the eyes, exploring space with the chin, and bobbing the head.

Hanging the lips slightly ajar and releasing the temporomandibular joint (aka the jaw) have a strong impact on the range of motion of the neck. Gibberish, speaking nonsensical words and sounds, encourages movement of the mouth in new and strange ways that can relax the face.

Try this:

With lips slightly parted, standing with a wide stance for stability, sweep both arms in a circle in front of you and follow your hands with your eyes. Do three circles in each direction. Notice how your head rotates on your neck as your eyes follow the rotation of your hands.

Archetype:

The Intuitive Power archetype is the owl. The owl is known for its connection to the mystery realms, the darkness of night where truth hides, that when revealed can bring light.

Music:

Music that brings us to the realm of Intuitive Power can be ethereal and trance-like or repetitive and percussive entraining our brainwaves into an altered state.

Playlist:

>Professor Trance and the Energizers "Become the Dance"
>Maneesh De Moor "Cosmic Flow"

Sense

In the texture of Sense you are dancing with your breath. The dance is light and spacious. Expansion and contraction of the limbs in time with the breath are a nice way to access the energy of Sense.

Try this:

Use music that evokes Sense. Lie comfortably on your back breathing fully and deeply in and out of your belly and your chest. Sensing inwardly, notice the subtle expansion and contraction of your chest, ribcage, shoulders, belly, and back. Begin to echo that expansion Begin to echo that expansion and contraction with your arms and legs, wrapping your arms around yourself and squeezing your knees into your chest as you exhale. Reach out away from your center as you inhale. Allow the motion to begin subtly at first, increasing the range of motion with each breath, so that eventually you're reaching out fully from your center and back again to your center as an expression of the dance of your breath. Let the dance morph into whatever your body feels most natural doing as you dance with your breath.

Music:

Music that inspires Sense is both ethereal and sensual inviting you inward to the realm of awareness of the less than tangible world. Instruments that induce this journey are voice that is breathy, string instruments like guitar and harp, and synthesized sounds.

Playlist:

>Enya *The Memory of Trees*
>Kitaro *The Light of the Spirit*

Movement Form:

Continuum Movement

Continuum uses movement, the dexterity of breath, the resonance of sound, and the value of meaning to amplify and refine a far-reaching communication within us, with others, and with our world. From http://www.continuummovement.com

Ground

In the texture of Ground you are dancing with your bones. This is a dense and earthy dance.

Try this:

Standing with a wider than hip stance, bend your knees and move your buttocks away from your knees. Lift one foot and both elbows (pointy part reaching upward and hands dropping toward earth) and then the other foot alternating from side to side. Let your shoulders be heavy rising with each foot lift and dropping each time you drop your foot back to the earth. Sense the sponginess in your knees and the heavy gravity-bound quality of your body and your dance.

Music:

Instruments that bring you into Ground are djembe and taiko drums.

Playlist:

Brent Lewis "Needy, Needy, Needy"
Madou Djembe "Energie"

Movement Form:

The style of dance that evokes Ground is African dance. While there are many styles of African dance that come from the many regions of this rich and diverse cultural continent, what they all share is consistent and sustained bending of the knees throughout the choreography to bring the tailbone and center of gravity just below the navel in closer relationship to the earth.

Mobilize

In Mobilize we dance with our fluids, blood, and lymph. The movements are characterized by spontaneity. They are erratic and free.

Try this:

Standing comfortably with feet about hip distance apart, knees spongy, mouth hanging open, shoulders relaxed, begin to shake. Let sound emerge from within you. Shake for at least three minutes. Pause and sense inward to the energy in motion within you.

Now, let that energy dance you!

Instruments that encourage Mobilize are clarinet, saxophone, marimba, bongos, and steel drums.

Playlist

>   Osho *Kundalini Meditation* "Track One"
>   Govinda "Inner Membrane"

Movement Form:

Salsa and karate

Harness

In Harness you dance with the membranous walls of your blood and lymph vessels. The motion is characterized by pulsing and squeezing.

Try this:

Starting with the dance of Sense above, using the music of Harness, move from the floating quality of Sense, making your movements faster and more sharply accentuated, grabbing outwardly and squeezing toward your core.

The instruments that evoke Harness are the combination of Mobilize and Ground:

Djembe and taiko drums, clarinet, saxophone, marimba, bongos, and steel drums.

Playlist:

> Blue Six "Sweeter Love"
> No Noise "Red Muladhara"

Movement Form:

Tai chi and aikido

Express

Combine all of the above and you have the elements of Express.

Try this:

Give yourself full permission to dance like no one is watching. Move from being the dancer to being the *dance*.

Playlist:

Basement Jaxx "Do Your Thing"
Rishi & Harshil "Forget Your Limitations"

Movement Form:

Ecstatic dance

Ecstatic dance takes you in the landscape of the shamanic state of consciousness through your mind and your body. Every cell in your body is humming with the state of reality. Your body, mind, and heart are collaboratively engaged, experiencing the context and contents of the journey as one.

Lenses

For all the practices below I recommend you choose music that is instrumental so the lyrics don't interfere with your self-inquiry.

Somatic Lens

With the Somatic Lens we are listening inwardly for sensation and are moved by what we perceive. We pay attention to impulse and surrender to its seduction to move the way it feels called to be moved. This can be a profoundly intimate practice that takes you into the inner truth dwelling in your tissues and gets you moving authentically and contemplatively.

Try this:

Using the *Tracking Sensation Exercise* from Chapter 11, begin by lying down and tracking sensation in your body that corresponds to the music you've chosen. Give yourself a few moments to just watch what's happening within you. Then begin to let the sensations be impulses to move. Let your body move in response to what it's sensing. If you lose track of the sensation, come back to stillness and start again. There's no right or wrong way to move here, only a felt Sense interaction between your awareness, your body sensation, your physical body, and the music.

Movement Form:

Authentic Movement

Authentic Movement is about trusting the innate wisdom of the body to lead us toward healing and the development of conscious presence. Practiced without music, the mover closes her eyes, waits, and then moves in response to body-felt sensations, emotions, memories, movement impulses, and/or images.

Creative Lens

Bring a question to your dance. When you're not able to move out of a situation that's causing you stress and struggle because the creative opportunity is not evident, devoting your dance or movement practice to your creative lens question can be a beautiful inquiry.

Try this:

Come to your practice with an intention to become consciously aware of the opportunity in a specific situation. Create the space by putting aside whatever might be a distraction. Stand with feet hip distance apart and begin with three grounding breaths. (Take a deep breath, reach out and up, and let your palms float down your midline facing the earth, to the ground. Repeat three times, each time dropping into your body and into the moment). On the final of four breaths, reach out and up; bring palms together and then down to your heart in prayer position. Offer your dance to the intention to come into conscious awareness of the opportunity for you in the current situation. Hold this intention throughout your dance, while staying open to the dance emerging freely as honest self-expression, unattached to form or the answer that arises.

Movement Form:

Expressive Arts Therapy

The premise of Expressive Arts Therapy is that art and its modes of expression including dance are a way to explore and support transformation through creativity and the imagination. Here we are focused on the process of creative expression rather than the outcome.

Spiritual Lens

I found dance through this lens. Dissolving self and merging with spirit through dance is the most intimate of journeys that I've known. This was such a rich place for me that it was a challenge to come back down to earth to relate with others through dance and interpersonal intimacy.

Try this:

I highly encourage your first explorations of the Spiritual Lens through dance to take place with an experienced and trusted guide. If this is not available to you, I suggest you create a safe and sacred space, free of obstacles and distractions, and experiment with moving to music with your eyes closed. Start with shorter explorations and lengthen the time of your practice as you become more comfortable and feel safer to both hold the space and immerse yourself in the dance. Devote your dance to being used by Source.

Movement Form:

Trance Dance

Trance Dance is practiced blindfolded. By dancing within the seclusion of darkness dancers enter a shamanic realm. In this *dance of the mystery* we can discover parallel realities where truths and awareness previously unconscious are made conscious. Through Trance Dance we disappear, becoming more like spirit, and simultaneously less attached to our typical way of seeing and interpreting life events.

CONCLUSION

A woman's way home, the journey to being true to yourself, will have you identifying and releasing all the ways you aren't. The habits of self-betrayal that have become second nature will melt away and you'll be able to claim the experience of feeling safe in your own body. This is an essential step in the direction of leadership that is infused with a sacred and sustainable quality, the cornerstone of embodied leadership and embodied power. As you claim this for yourself, taste its potency to make a difference for others, and ache to make it available to them, you will have moved into the realm of sacred activism.

Something as simple as *being true* seems like it should be simple to live. Unfortunately, that's not the case. If it were, I wouldn't have felt the calling to spend years of my life devoted to this work.

On a reunion call with one of my groups after a week together in Mexico, I shared that we have spent so much of our life abandoning our own body, it's no wonder that when we drop in and spend some time really being with our embodied self, it can take some getting used to. All our relationships will be touched by our newfound embodied way of being. When we come home to our true soul essence and simmer in that *being home*, it can feel threatening when others who don't know us that way interact with our newness. There may be a tendency to over-boundary ourselves, to be careful with our energy and its expression or to simply not know how to relate from this new place of loyalty to self over loyalty to other.

If the ideas and practices in this book have found their way into your body, heart, and soul, and inspired even a few aha's pertaining to what you're dancing in your life, you may experience some or all of the above. As you launch yourself on your unique path to embodied power or continue your journey that started many moons ago, what's most vital is that you honor that journey as unique, release expectations, and open to the wonder of living in a body and the mystery inherent in that.

There is no ETA (estimated time of arrival) at fully certified embodiment. Home, it turns out is not a destination after all, but an experiential state of being and the adventure of constantly finding our poise on the crest of that being. You are the heroine of your own odyssey, your consciousness expanding with each moment of embodied presence and tender self-care. What you *can* expect is that the more aware you become, the more you'll be sensitive to when you're not in your body, and be able to bring yourself back home.

The privilege of awareness can frustrate and confuse you because you'll see yourself fragmenting, when after all this time of devoted work you thought you'd be able to sustain wholeness and integration of all parts of your being. In the awareness, and the frustration, and confusion that accompanies it, that is when all you can do is return to your beautiful body temple, ask yourself where within you you're sensing the frustration and confusion, and trust that marinating there *is* the way home. Compassion, patience, and humor will all be precious allies on this adventure so acquaint yourself intimately with these for the ride of your life and dive into the home you embody, navigating the way, your way, dancing, divining and loving your way there.

ABOUT THE AUTHOR

Leela Francis is an international facilitator, therapist, coach and sacred activist. She expertly weaves movement, dance, sacred circle and ritual as explorative vehicles for psycho-spiritual expansion. She's devoted her life to discovering as much as possible about the topic of human embodiment and women's awakening as tools for planetary peace and personal healing.

The founder of Vividly Woman Embodied Leader Tools and Trainings, Leela facilitates Vividly Woman events all over North America and in Mexico and appears as a facilitator and speaker at other live and virtual events. Passionate about women's right to embodied freedom, she founded the Daily Dance at Home-A-Thon and Sensual Heart programs to raise awareness and funds for women survivors of war by encouraging women to dance for our sisters globally.

When she's not teaching or attending to her business, she's running and dancing on the beach in Mexico or on an adventure with her husband, Greg, and Redbone Coonhound, Bailey Bob.

THE VIVIDLY WOMAN EXPERIENCE

Are you ready to claim the embodied and powerful Vividly Woman version of YOU?

Dance with us to radiantly expand your personal integrity, life fulfillment, and joyfilled vibrancy.

Now that you've learned the basics of the Vividly Woman Solar System it's time to enjoy genuine and juicy embodiment. Leela and the Vividly Woman Team will guide you to make love to your life so that you're living a deliciously divine existence NOW. Not some day, one day, when and if umpteen numbers of other conditions are in place, NOW!

Our secret formula includes:

- Getting you connected to a conscious community of sisters devoted to embodied feminine power,
- Providing you with the tools and training that will support you loving and living in your body,
- Starting you off with a one-on-one *Live in Your Body* coaching session with a certified Vividly Woman Embodied Leader Coach.

Find out more about our *Woman's Way Home Get Connected* package at the link below and insert the code **Home at Last to get a 50% discount** off the regular package price.

ARE YOU READY TO MAKE LOVE TO YOUR LIFE?

Let's get you home to the Vividly Woman You! We are here to take you by the hand and together claim what all women truly deserve and desire!

Call us at
1-800-388-6514
Or contact us at
www.VividlyWoman.com/get-connected

VIVIDLY WOMAN AT YOUR EVENT

Do you have an upcoming live or virtual event where you'd like to share the message of women's empowerment: body, self, and soul?

Do you want to get your audience out of their heads, into their bodies, and integrating your teachings for greater impact, deeper understanding, and sustained results?

Invite Leela Francis to bring a Vividly Woman embodied leadership keynote, workshop or presentation to your event, retreat or seminar.

> *Leela and her Vividly Woman Embodiment teachings amped up the impact of my recent Genius Rockstar Retreat immeasurably. The participants felt immediately safe to express themselves fully through movement. They LOVED it and also went to deep and healing places that would not have been possible without Leela's guidance. She lovingly offered each of the participants laser insights on how to embody their power. Along with the safe and sacred container that she creates, they were able to integrate my curriculum beyond what I even hoped for. Thank you Leela for sharing your genius so generously!*
>
> Karen Evelyn www.LiveYourGenius.com

> *"Leela is awesome! She's a uniquely dynamic and inspirational contribution to our pro- grams. Our participants adore her heart opening and joyful blend of the sacred and the sensual, eliciting purpose and passion, and a profound experience of personal expansion."*
>
> - T. Harv Eker, NY Times #1 Best-selling Author of Secrets of the Millionaire Mind

We're also happy to explore co-producing a Vividly Woman training in your area.

Contact us at
www.leelafrancis.com/site/contact

SUGGESTED READING

Sensual Power

Desilets, Saida. *Emergence of the Sensual Woman: Awakening Our Erotic Innocence. Jade Goddess Pub., 2006*

McIntyre, Julie. *Sex and the Intelligence of the Heart: Nature, Intimacy, and Sexual Energy. VT:* Destiny Books, 2012

Emotional Power

Comstock, Kami and Thame, Marisa. *Journey Into Love: Ten Steps to Wholeness. NY:* Willow Press, 2000

Lerner, Harriet. *The Dance of Intimacy.* NY: HarperCollins, 1989

Intuitive Power

Andrews, Lynn. *Woman on the Edge of Two Worlds.* NY: Harper Perennial, 1994

Trumpa, Chögyam. *Cutting Through Spiritual Materialism*, MA: Shamabala Pub., 1973

Sense

Rosas, Debbie and Rosas, Carlos. *The Nia Technique: The High-Powered Energizing Workout that Gives You a New Body and a New Life. NY:* Three Rivers Press, 2005

Rosenberg Ph.D., Jack Lee and Kitaen-Morse Ph.D, Beverly. *The Intimate Couple.* Turner Publishing, 1996

Ground

Abram, David. *The Spell of the Sensuous.* NY: Vintage Books, 1997

Farhi, Donna. *Yoga Mind, Body & Spirit: A Return to Wholeness.* NY: Holt, 2000

Mobilize

Chermak McElroy, Susan. *Heart In the Wild. NY:* Ballantine Books, 2003

Halifax, Joan. *The Fruitful Darkness*, San Francisco: Harper, 1994

Harness

Ford, Debbie. *The Dark Side of the Light Chasers. NY: Riverhead, 1999*

Zweig, Connie and Wolf, Steven. *Romancing the Shadow: A Guide to Soul Work for a Vital, Authentic Life. NY: Wellspring/Ballantine, 1999*

Express

Abelar, Taisha, and Castaneda, Carlos *The Sorcerer's Crossing. NY:* Penguin Books, 1992

Cameron, Julia. *The Artist's Way.* NY: Tarcher/Putnam, 1992

Somatic Lens

Hartley, Linda. *Wisdom of the Body Moving: An Introduction to Body-Mind Centering.* North Atlantic Books, 1989

Hutchison, Marcia Germaine. *Transforming Body Image: Learning to Love the Body You Have.* The Crossing Press, 1985

Creative Lens

Estes, Clarissa Pinkola. *The Creative Fire.* Audio CD. Louisville, CO: Sounds True, 2005

Halprin, Anna. *Returning to Health: With Dance, Movement & Imagery.* Mendocino, CA: Liferhythm, 2002

Spiritual Lens

Estes, Clarissa Pinkola. *Women Who Run with the Wolves.* NY: Random House, 1995

Lucia, Rene. *Unplugging the Patriarchy: A Mystical Journey Into the Heart of the New Age.* Crown Chakra Pub, 2009

General Reading

Barks, Coleman. *Naked Song.* Maypop, 1992

Cohen, Michael. *Web of Life Imperative.* Bloomfield, IN: Trafford Pub, 2003

Heartfield, Joan. *Romancing the Beloved.* Cool, CA: Talking Hearts, 2010

Kidd, Sue Monk. *Dance Of the Dissident Daughter.* NY: Harper One, 1996

Lindemans, Micha, Ed. *Encyclopedia Mythica*. www.pantos.org/atw/welcome.hmtl 2002

Roth, Geneen. *Breaking Free from Emotional Eating*, NY: Penguin, 2004

Rust, Ezra Gardner. *The Music and Dance of the World's Religions*. Westport, CT: Greenwood Pub, 1996

Shinoda, Jean Bolen. *The Millionth Circle: How to Change Ourselves and the World—The Essential Guide to Woman's Circle*. Berkeley, CA: Conari Press, 1999. *Urgent Message from Mother: Gather the Women Save the World*. Berkeley, CA: Conari Press, 2005

Sinek, Simon. *Start With Why*. NY: Portfolio: 2009

Stewart, Iris J. *Sacred Woman, Sacred Dance: Awakening Spirituality Through Movement and Ritual. VT:* Inner Traditions, 2000

Woodman, Marion and Mellick, Jill. *Coming Home to Myself: Reflections for Nurturing a Woman's Body and Soul*. Berkeley, CA: Conari Press, 1998

SUPPORT RESOURCES

Sexual Abuse

www.aftersilence.org/index.php
www.ascasupport.org

Eating Disorders

www.nationaleatingdisorders.org/find-help-support
www.eatingdisordersanonymous.org

Eco-therapy

www.ecopsychology.org
www.joannamacy.net

Expressive Arts Therapy

www.tamalpa.org/index.html
www.ieata.org

Spiritual Sexual Education

www.divine-feminine.com
www.sourcetantra.com

Women's Advocacy and Aid

www.womenthrive.org
www.womenforwomen.org
www.womenscentersintl.org

The Vividly Woman Solar System

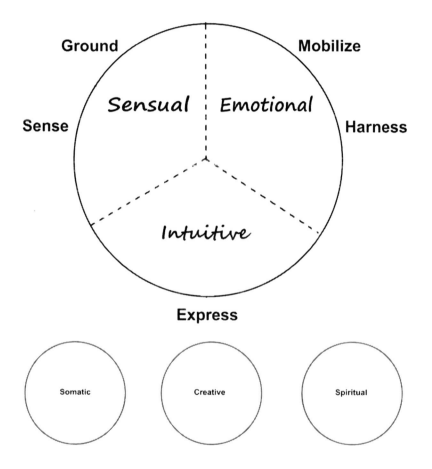

INDEX

A

Abandonment 102, 136
Abuse xx, 11, 43, 51, 56, 67, 174, 176, 188, 208, 237
Action 10, 13, 33, 40, 46, 47, 51, 70, 114, 125, 128, 130, 134, 136, 139, 141–143, 163, 171, 179, 183, 201, 202, 204
Activist 46, 50, 87, 115, 207, 227
  Sensual Power Activist 46
Addiction 62, 148–150, 164
Aliveness xxii, 4, 7, 14, 24, 29, 32, 34, 37, 46, 50, 55, 59, 92, 139, 160, 189, 196, 203
Anger 122, 132, 154, 193
Anna Halprin 178
Anxiety xxi, 52, 96, 130, 140, 149
Archetype 30, 46–48, 59, 67, 72, 88, 125, 152, 181, 212–214
Arousal 25, 30, 33, 35, 36, 42, 73, 77, 212
Authenticity 59, 94, 114, 154, 164
Awakening xii, xxiii, 2, 33, 60, 74, 88, 92, 106, 108, 119, 123, 134, 135, 158, 169, 175, 177, 189, 191, 192, 196, 202, 205, 206, 208, 227, 233, 236
Awareness xii, xiii, xxvi, 8, 10, 11, 15, 22, 30, 34, 36, 45–47, 51, 54, 57, 62–64, 66, 68–70, 73, 74, 76, 78, 80, 82, 84–87, 91–94, 94, 96, 98, 102, 103, 108–111, 114, 116, 118, 121, 127, 128, 133, 135, 151, 153, 167, 171, 182, 189, 191, 193, 196, 201, 207, 208, 211, 216, 221–223, 226, 227

B

Balance 29, 57, 111, 139, 162, 201
Belief xiii, 40, 122, 200, 209
Beloved 75, 125, 157, 235
Blame 43, 54, 66, 78, 96, 101, 122, 138, 193–195
Body 129, 234
Boundaries 102, 102–106, 108, 122, 153–155, 160, 164, 177, 208
Brain 52, 72–74, 92
Breath 31, 154, 197, 215, 216, 222
Business 2, 11, 44, 64, 65, 67, 71, 72, 123, 138, 141, 143, 149, 163, 164, 181, 193, 201, 202, 227

C

Carry xiii, 6, 37, 38, 43, 111, 116
Celebration xxii, 13, 135, 166, 168, 175, 182, 183
Chakras 7
Channel 51, 76, 81, 86
Child 43, 61, 69, 84, 116, 122, 135, 152, 188, 206, 207
Chin 214
Choice 8, 22, 34, 39, 49, 53, 57, 70, 71, 79, 81, 83, 84, 98, 112, 123, 125,

131, 146, 147, 152, 153, 163, 174, 177, 179, 188, 189, 202
Circle xiii, xviii, xxiii, xxv, 1, 2, 28, 29, 42, 53, 57, 61, 74, 75, 84, 96, 104, 111, 140, 160, 167–170, 174, 187, 188, 214, 227, 236
Claiming 7, 19, 47, 75, 76, 88, 99
Clarissa Pinkola Estes 12, 203
Commitment 129, 142, 161
Communion 23, 93, 94, 142
Connect 4, 21, 22, 24, 71, 74, 76, 86, 94, 102, 104, 112, 114, 118, 119, 121, 136, 202, 205, 209, 229
Connection 1, 11, 20, 23, 26, 35, 37, 38, 42, 45, 48, 52, 61, 73, 74, 77, 79, 81, 92, 93, 99, 102, 103, 105, 111, 112, 113–115, 117, 118, 120, 127, 136, 141, 158, 175, 208, 212, 213, 214
Consciousness xix, 10, 11, 26, 39, 40, 54, 56, 60, 66, 72, 73, 75, 76, 121, 135, 157, 177, 188, 191, 192, 196, 205, 208, 220, 226
Contain 29, 77, 111, 153, 158, 164
Container xiii, 99, 104, 109, 111, 112, 149, 158
Continuum 8, 9, 76, 91, 166, 196, 216
Contracted 35, 105, 145, 156, 202
Control 64, 111, 123, 147, 202
Craving 29, 35, 35–37, 47, 55, 74, 202
Creativity 28, 139, 140, 203, 204, 222
Crone 46, 72, 82, 88, 181

D

Dance xii, xiv, xviii, xix, xx, xxii, xxvii, 5, 7–9, 15, 23, 36, 39–41, 44, 51, 58, 60, 70, 74, 75, 78, 79, 92, 96, 105, 115, 119, 129, 134–136, 140, 144, 145, 149, 151, 153, 158–160, 162, 167, 172, 173, 175, 178, 182, 188, 192, 196, 197, 200, 201, 205, 210, 215–223, 227, 229, 233, 235, 236

Dancing xxiii, 23, 28, 30, 35, 40, 68, 108, 116, 125, 134–136, 167, 173, 197, 210, 215, 216, 223, 226, 227
Decision 60, 64, 65, 79–84, 87, 98, 101, 179
Demeter 124, 125
Denial 146
Depression xxi, 13, 52, 130
Devotion xv, xvi, xvii, xviii, 72, 106, 128–130, 142, 145, 154, 161, 168, 169, 180, 188
Digestion 51, 53, 54
Disease 44, 52, 124, 178, 182, 193, 198
Drama 39, 56, 60, 65, 112
Dyads 9

E

Earth 1, 4, 24, 30, 36, 46, 47, 87, 94, 110–112, 114, 117, 119, 120–122, 124, 125, 162, 212, 217, 222
Eco-therapy 9, 24, 237
Ecstasy 22, 134, 142, 175
Ego 14, 68, 69, 69–72, 79, 83, 84, 87, 179, 180, 205, 206
Elbow 213, 216
Embodied xii, xix, xx, xxii, xxiii, 2, 4, 12, 14, 15, 20, 34, 37, 43, 48, 50, 67, 73, 78, 88, 102, 105, 106, 109, 113, 123, 125, 127, 134, 143, 151, 159, 165, 166, 176, 182, 187, 188, 190, 192, 196, 198, 202, 204, 209, 211, 225–227, 229, 231
Embodiment xix, xxi, xxii, xxiii, xxv, xxvi, 8, 12, 13, 15, 45, 91, 134, 173, 187, 191, 210, 226, 227, 229
Emotional xiii, xiv, 4, 7, 8, 13, 15, 21, 37, 47, 49, 50, 51, 52, 53, 54, 55, 56, 58, 59, 60, 63, 64, 65, 66, 67, 68, 73, 78, 91, 101, 121, 137, 138, 139, 140, 144, 148, 151, 152, 153, 159, 172, 176, 178, 188, 191, 199, 212, 213, 233, 236

Emotions 4, 41, 49–53, 53, 53–59, 62–64, 66–68, 72, 74, 77, 97, 101, 121, 132, 139, 140, 144, 145, 164, 195, 213, 221
Empathy xii, 50, 51, 55, 61, 93
Empower xvii, 19, 34, 144, 151
Erogenous 4, 73, 74, 92
Essence xi, xii, xv, xviii, 9, 10, 13, 24, 29, 35, 36, 42, 56, 59, 65, 97, 106, 110, 111, 114, 117, 118, 127, 128, 140–143, 161, 163, 169, 181, 205, 207, 208, 225
Expanded 105, 118, 127, 145, 149, 151, 152, 154–156, 164
Expansion xii, xxi, xxii, 139, 144, 148, 149, 150, 153, 158, 165, 200, 215, 227
Express 8, 15, 27, 36, 37, 44, 47, 49, 51, 53, 56–59, 64, 67, 75, 85, 86, 91, 119, 121, 137, 139, 145, 146, 159, 166, 167, 171, 172, 174, 177–182, 219, 234
Expression xii, xxiii, 4, 7, 14, 24, 26, 27, 37, 45, 46, 48, 51, 53, 56, 57, 67, 103, 105, 108, 121, 122, 125, 140, 154, 158, 162, 166, 168, 169, 171, 172, 174, 175, 178–181, 183, 193, 208, 215, 222, 226
Expressive arts 51, 178, 222, 237

F

Family xv, 50, 68, 69, 78, 79, 113, 115, 116, 123, 132, 153, 156, 202, 208
Fear xi, xiii, 2, 11, 30, 40, 43, 63, 80, 81, 82, 83, 105, 140, 149, 152, 171, 175, 180, 200
Feelings xi, 22, 49, 50, 55–58, 61–63, 67, 74, 81, 97, 112, 136, 141, 144, 148, 150, 172, 174, 193, 194, 195, 195–198
Feminine xxiii, 4, 7, 13, 14, 26–29, 42, 47, 50, 73, 76, 107, 130, 142, 143, 159, 160, 160–162, 165, 176, 188–191, 229, 238
Fitness 20, 21, 21–23, 47
Fixed 105, 156
Flirting 24, 25, 26, 119
Flow 4, 29, 35, 91, 105, 122, 132, 140, 156, 159, 160, 173, 195, 212, 215
Fluid 105, 156, 161, 212, 217
Foundation 33, 42, 91, 102
Freedom xv, 49, 50, 56, 59, 91, 104, 122, 123, 125, 140, 161, 169, 172, 174, 175, 199, 211, 212, 227
Fruition 91
Fulfillment xxi, 3, 29, 36, 46, 47, 77, 79, 130, 135, 136, 167, 189, 229

G

Gaia 23, 162
God 36, 55, 58, 74, 76, 85, 134, 194
Goddess 30, 46–48, 57–59, 58, 67, 71, 72, 76, 87, 88, 106, 123, 124, 125, 135, 141, 162, 180, 233
    Express Goddess 180
    Ground Goddess 124
    Harness Goddess 162
    Sense Goddess 106
Grief xx, 35, 55, 135, 136, 137, 173, 201
Ground 8–10, 15, 45, 48, 91, 96, 110, 110–114, 117, 120–125, 125–127, 137, 141, 144, 148, 153, 158–160, 163, 166, 195, 196, 212, 216, 217, 219, 222, 234
Growth xiv, xxii, 22, 29, 39, 87, 114, 132, 149, 163, 169, 171, 200–203
G-spot 176

H

Harness 6, 8, 10, 15, 27, 36, 50, 65, 91, 106, 112, 137, 139, 144–147, 151–153, 157–159, 159–166, 165,

178, 179, 182, 190, 192, 208, 218, 219, 234
Harnessing 27, 37, 48, 56, 144, 145, 148, 153, 154, 158, 163, 164
Head 4, 8, 11, 12, 25, 27, 39, 50, 56, 60, 69, 97, 101, 117, 124, 138, 179, 193–196, 214, 231
Healing xii, xiv, xvii, xx, 35, 39, 51, 55, 74, 75, 76, 76–79, 115, 118, 119, 123, 134, 154, 157, 175, 176, 178, 201, 205, 206, 208, 221, 227
Heart xiii, xvi, xviii, xx, xxii, 4, 8, 23, 25, 26, 36, 50, 57, 58, 64, 65, 69, 73, 91, 94, 101, 118–120, 128–130, 132, 135, 138, 139, 141–144, 152, 159, 172, 173, 177, 199, 200, 203, 212, 213, 220, 222, 226, 227, 233–235
Holding space xxii
Home xi, xii, xiii, xiv, xx, xxii, 6, 12, 14, 27, 43, 45, 60, 68, 75, 78, 93, 98, 104, 105, 108, 110–113, 113, 114–116, 118, 119, 126, 131, 142, 145, 163, 168, 169, 177, 180, 182, 190, 207, 211, 225–227, 229, 236
Homesickness xii
Humility 202, 204

I

Icons 107, 125, 141
    Mobilize Icons 141
    Sense Icons 107
Image 27, 38, 55, 135, 140, 187, 221, 235
Imagination 92, 95, 199, 203, 222
Infertility xii, 115
Insight xiii, xxi, xxiii, xxvi, 2, 8, 11, 13, 15, 62, 65, 70, 74, 85, 101, 120, 188, 190, 192, 198, 211
Integration 12, 15, 226

Integrity 14, 44, 51, 52, 59, 64, 72, 79, 81–83, 86, 87, 94, 123, 137, 154, 164, 181, 229
Intelligence 21, 23, 86, 172, 192, 233
Intention 21, 22, 65, 69, 81, 119, 137, 222
Intimacy xxii, 2, 23, 24, 43, 50, 52, 66, 77, 94, 102, 114, 123, 136, 154, 157, 164, 166, 175, 183, 207, 222, 233
Intuition 68, 69, 69–72, 74, 79–81, 82–87, 130, 179, 180, 183, 192, 198, 205
Intuitive 4, 8, 15, 50, 62, 63, 68, 70, 72, 73, 74, 76, 79, 80, 81, 82, 83, 85, 86, 87, 88, 91, 179, 180, 191, 205, 214, 215, 233

J

Jean Bolen xvii, 236
Journey xi, xii, xvi, xxii, xxvi, 2, 41, 44, 49, 76, 91, 108, 117, 119, 120, 125, 127, 142, 151, 166–168, 178, 181, 187, 189, 196, 200, 202, 211, 216, 220, 222, 225, 226, 233, 235
Joy 20, 43, 55, 129, 136, 175, 183
Judgment xi, 6, 11, 38, 101, 112, 113, 136, 154, 174, 175

K

Knee xiii, 120, 211, 212, 215–218
Knowing 4, 22, 25, 55, 76, 77, 79, 83, 103, 113, 114, 118, 135, 138, 139, 174, 178

L

Lateral 189
Leader xii, xxii, xxiii, 2, 14, 15, 34, 46, 50, 78, 102, 105, 106, 122, 123, 151, 176, 227, 229

Leaking 37, 48, 150, 164
Light xi, xii, xvi, xviii, 22, 37–42, 44, 47, 62, 85, 88, 98, 121, 136, 156, 158, 175, 178, 208, 214–216, 234
Linear 8, 27, 99, 130, 189
Longing xi, xii, xviii, 26, 35, 36, 45, 55, 74
Love xi, xiii, xviii, xix, xxi, 9, 22–24, 28, 35, 37, 41, 42, 50, 55, 66, 76, 83, 94, 105, 110, 111, 130, 132, 139, 141, 143, 148, 149, 153, 157, 161, 168, 176, 180, 194, 196, 198, 207, 213, 219, 229, 233, 235

M

Maiden 46, 59, 67, 124, 125
Manipulation 56, 67
Margaret Thatcher 125
Marilyn Monroe 107
Marriage 60, 61, 77, 78, 85
Masculine 27, 27–29, 47, 50, 130, 160, 161, 162, 165, 189, 191
Maturity 65, 178, 188
Meaning xv, xvii, 1, 14, 27, 40, 51, 65, 74, 104, 105, 111, 117, 128, 130, 130–133, 136, 138, 139, 139–143, 153, 159, 168, 189, 195, 216
Meditation 197, 218
Mental 21, 47, 52, 60, 72–74, 95, 101, 146
Mind xvi, xix, xx, xxii, 2, 12, 27, 38, 43, 52, 56, 61, 63, 69, 70, 72–74, 79, 82, 83, 87, 92, 94, 101, 112, 118, 124, 139, 140, 168, 177, 179, 182, 193, 195, 196, 220, 234, 235
Mirror 24, 38, 48, 106, 189, 192
Mobilize 8, 10, 15, 65, 91, 123, 128, 130, 134, 137, 139, 141, 142–144, 158, 159, 166, 179, 217–219, 234
Money 11, 144, 145, 149, 152, 153
Mood 34, 57–59, 58, 103

Mother xviii, 30, 32, 39, 46–48, 52, 66, 71, 84, 94, 111, 117, 123–126, 138, 140, 147, 152, 162, 171, 177, 188, 202, 207, 236
Mystical 136, 235

N

Nature xx, 14, 20, 23, 24, 24–26, 28, 29, 37, 46, 69, 80, 93, 94, 119–121, 122, 127, 130, 136, 142, 143, 145, 154, 160, 161, 188, 205, 208, 225, 233
Numinous 136

O

Objectification 24, 121
Oneness 24, 111, 117, 118, 205
Opportunity xvi, xx, 12, 13, 57, 93, 131, 163, 189, 200, 201, 203, 221, 222
Oprah 71, 162
Oshun 106

P

Pain xi, xiii, xv, xx, 12, 30, 39, 40, 43, 52, 53, 55, 58, 60, 61, 77, 78, 101, 136, 150, 173–177, 183, 200
Paradigm xxii, 44, 46, 142, 143
Passion xix, xx, xxi, 14, 32, 87, 162, 180, 181
Patriarchal 29, 42, 44, 54
Peace 3, 14, 23, 29, 34, 55, 72, 81–83, 87, 102, 136, 151, 189, 194, 227
Pele 181
Pelvis 4
Permission 7, 30, 32, 47, 52, 169, 194, 195, 198, 219
Persephone 124
Personal xii, xxi, xxii, 8, 13, 14, 42, 44, 50, 60, 64, 74, 76, 81–83, 88, 102, 119, 132, 138, 141, 153, 158,

169, 190, 200, 201, 203, 206, 207, 227, 229
Physical xx, 14, 19, 20, 21, 22, 30, 33, 35, 39, 47, 49, 75, 82, 103, 104, 111–114, 118, 121, 127, 152, 176, 191–193, 221
Pleasure xx, 7, 19, 20, 31–35, 37, 42, 47, 52, 74, 129, 154–156
Porous 156
Potential 4, 7, 11, 30, 31, 34, 37, 39, 42, 50, 52, 64–66, 101, 176
Power xvi, xx, xxi, xxii, 4, 6, 7, 8, 12, 14, 15, 23, 26, 30, 32, 33, 34, 37, 39, 40, 41, 43, 44, 45, 47, 48, 49, 50, 54, 55, 59, 61, 64, 66, 67, 68, 70, 73, 74, 76, 78, 79, 87, 88, 91, 104, 105, 109, 113, 119, 121, 123, 127, 131, 143, 144, 145, 149, 154, 156, 158, 159, 161, 163, 164, 165, 171, 178, 180, 182, 183, 187, 188, 189, 190, 192, 198, 204, 209, 211, 214, 225, 226, 229
Practice xxv, 9, 13, 20, 21, 22–24, 26, 31, 36, 42, 57, 58, 73, 77, 78, 85, 97, 99, 101, 106, 111, 114, 116, 123, 132–135, 144, 146, 154, 158, 163, 166, 168, 174, 176, 177, 181, 182, 192, 194–198, 201, 202, 208, 220–223, 226
Presence xv, xix, 25, 58, 72, 92, 96, 110, 112, 114, 117, 126–128, 154, 202, 204, 207, 221, 226
Procrastination 178, 180
Professional 44, 50, 71, 102
Purpose xv, 8, 73, 78, 95, 136, 139, 143, 150, 180, 204, 206, 207, 209

Q

Quality xii, 9, 10, 13, 14, 29, 42, 44, 50, 58, 83, 84, 92, 94, 96, 99, 102, 103, 108, 117, 120, 121, 127, 142, 160, 161, 174, 192, 204, 205, 217, 218, 225

R

Reaction 35, 45, 74, 106, 123, 171, 195
Rebirth xi
Recapitulation 167, 168, 170, 182
Reciprocity 112, 119
Rejection 11, 43, 148
Relationship xii, xiii, xviii, 6, 14, 15, 19, 20, 24, 30, 42, 45, 47, 57, 60, 61, 63–65, 67, 70, 72, 80, 85, 91, 96–98, 102, 103, 105–108, 111, 112, 114, 117, 119, 120, 123–125, 131, 140–142, 145–147, 152–155, 164, 175, 182, 187, 188, 196, 217, 225
Resonance 30, 45, 47, 99, 216
Responsibility 54, 60, 64, 188
Ritual xx, 40, 69, 78, 135, 151, 168, 173, 188, 227, 236

S

Sacred xi, xiii, xvii, xx, xxiii, xxvii, 1, 2, 6, 29, 32, 42, 61, 74, 78, 93, 111, 117, 135, 140, 174, 176, 188, 192, 206, 223, 225, 227, 236
Sadness 30, 57, 60, 141, 193
Safety 80, 170, 182
Sculptural 13, 130
Self xi, xii, xiii, xxi, xxii, 8–10, 13, 14, 20, 21, 27, 29, 37, 39, 45, 52, 53, 56, 60, 63–66, 68–70, 72, 73, 79, 83, 87, 94, 101–103, 106, 108, 110, 112, 114, 117, 121, 122, 123, 129, 132, 136, 138, 140, 148–151, 154, 157, 159, 161, 162, 164, 168, 174–176, 178, 180, 183, 187–189, 192–195, 200, 201, 205, 206, 208, 214, 220, 222, 226, 231
Self-discovery 13, 45, 129

Self-esteem 39, 136, 138, 148
Self-inquiry 8, 187, 220
Self-love 168, 194
Self-referring 94, 108
Self-respect 45
Self-sabotage 148, 150, 164
Self-worth 37, 39, 83, 136, 149, 201
Sensation 5, 8, 22, 30, 33, 34, 38, 47, 49, 55, 56, 63, 73, 84, 92, 94, 97, 98, 102, 108, 112, 114, 149, 166, 173, 174, 189, 192–198, 203, 220, 221
Sense xi, xiii, xv, xxi, 2, 8, 9, 13, 15, 19, 19–25, 27, 30, 31, 33, 35–39, 42, 45, 47, 53, 57–59, 69, 71, 81, 85, 91–97, 97, 97–100, 102–113, 117–121, 127–129, 130, 136, 144, 149, 153–155, 161, 163, 166–168, 172–174, 182, 193–195, 213, 215–218, 221, 234
Sense icons 107
Sensual xx, 4, 7, 8, 19, 20, 22, 23, 28, 29, 32, 33, 36, 37, 40, 43, 44, 45, 47, 70, 73, 77, 92, 93, 95, 99, 106, 107, 115, 119, 134, 142, 159, 189, 196, 216
Sensuality xx, 27, 29, 33, 37, 42, 45, 96, 106, 107, 161, 188
Sexuality 4, 19, 24, 37, 42, 47, 147, 157, 176, 188, 192
Shadow xi, 37–42, 43, 46, 48, 52, 57, 62, 63, 85, 121–123, 127, 136, 137, 139, 148, 150–153, 158, 159, 164, 174, 177, 234
Shamanic 39, 116, 151, 220, 223
Shame xiii, 37, 38, 41–43, 148, 169, 172, 173, 174, 176, 182
Sister xi, xx, xxiii, 6, 7, 28, 29, 32, 40, 43, 57, 61, 75, 76, 79, 80, 84, 107, 110, 112, 117, 122, 137, 162, 174, 180, 227, 229
Sisterhood xi, xv, xviii

Solar System 2, 4, 10, 14, 15, 45, 91, 102, 134, 138, 159, 210, 229
Soul xi, xii, xiii, xvi, xviii, xix, xx, xxi, xxii, 3, 23, 45, 55, 64, 71, 110, 120, 129, 130, 138, 144, 151, 176, 203, 225, 226, 231, 234, 236
Source 14, 23, 30, 37, 47, 55, 74, 78, 79, 86, 92, 114, 118, 121, 180, 197, 223
Sourcing 21, 84, 101, 194, 198
Spirit 11, 12, 21, 73, 76, 78, 101, 111, 113, 114, 118, 119, 132, 134, 149, 205, 208, 209, 216, 222, 223, 234
Spirituality xx, 21, 206, 236
Starhawk 87
Stimulation 92, 98, 139
Story xiii, xxiii, 12, 33, 51, 56, 57, 60, 60–62, 97, 116, 122–124, 125, 127, 140, 146, 148, 151, 153, 178, 194, 195, 198, 206, 207
Subconscious 41, 58, 148, 164, 178
Suffering xii, xiii, xx, xxi, xxii, 11, 13, 14, 34, 52, 54, 60, 60–63, 66, 69, 97, 106, 137, 138, 159, 174, 194
Suppression 39, 51, 52
Surrender 25, 35, 111, 113, 158, 220
Sustain 22, 130, 139, 143, 144, 150, 151, 160, 163, 165, 226

T

Tantra 158
Tara 141
Temple 13, 19, 20, 38, 49, 71, 79, 111, 114, 127, 145, 191, 226
Therapy 9, 24, 36, 98, 104, 112, 147, 178, 222, 237
Tracking 196, 197, 221
Trance 9, 39, 135, 215, 223
Trauma 56, 176
Trust 72, 82, 87, 105, 115, 123, 137, 153, 202, 226

Truth xi, xiii, xviii, xxi, xxii, 12–14, 20, 21, 22, 32, 38, 42, 44, 45, 48, 50, 55, 56, 60, 61, 68, 69, 80–82, 85–87, 94, 98, 101, 104, 108, 111–114, 122, 124, 125, 148, 150, 151, 166, 168–171, 174, 181, 182, 191–193, 196, 199, 202, 214, 220

U

Understanding xix, xxi, 2, 12, 15, 24, 29, 77, 91, 92, 99, 108, 135, 187, 210, 231

V

Vibration 99
Victim xv, xx, 54, 58, 60, 78, 132, 178, 195
VividExistence 99
Voice 21, 41, 69, 70, 72, 80, 81, 85–87, 140, 175, 192, 216
Vulnerability 2, 139

W

Waiting 24, 179, 180, 183
Web strings 24, 26, 76
Weight 30, 36, 41, 43, 117, 145–148
Well-being xxi, 7, 24, 27, 37, 44, 50, 55, 103, 114, 129
Wisdom xii, xiii, xvi, xvii, xix, xx, xxi, xxii, xxv, 2, 4, 7, 10–13, 17, 21, 24, 35, 41, 45, 54, 64, 68, 70, 73, 74, 76, 79, 80, 82, 86, 114, 141, 145, 152, 159, 179, 185, 187, 189, 192, 202, 205, 208, 213, 214, 221, 235
Witness xiii, 25, 51, 55, 57, 58, 64, 66, 67, 72, 73, 75, 112, 121, 122, 168, 175, 177, 178
Witnessing 56, 57, 80, 82, 189
Womb xviii, 31, 117, 206

Work xii, xiv, xx, xxvi, 2, 4, 14, 19, 23, 27, 29, 32, 40, 41, 44, 51, 64, 65, 71, 75–77, 76–77, 82, 99, 101, 103, 104, 112, 138, 140, 145, 146, 149, 150, 154, 156, 159, 163, 175, 181, 194, 201–203, 206, 225, 226, 234
Emotional Power at work 64
Sensual Power at Work 44

Y

Yoga 23, 36, 111, 154, 166, 167, 192, 234

CPSIA information can be obtained at www.ICGtesting.com
Printed in the USA
BVOW03s0926100714

358687BV00002B/3/P